AF488810

God Is God

God Is Not A Man

Mary L. Lyon

Library of Congress Control Number: 2016905870
CreateSpace Independent Publishing Platform
North Charleston, SC

rev. date 9/13/2016

CONTENTS

DEDICATION

This book is dedicated to everyone who has struggled with the maleness of God. It is hoped that you will be able to see God with new eyes and a new heart. He is so worthy of our love and devotion.

ACKNOWLEDGEMENT

In every endeavor, there are those who labor in love to support those of us who pursue our dreams. Those who have labored in love with me bless me. Each of them shared their gifts to help me.

NB - You continually lift me up and encourage me. As you share what God is doing in your life, I grow.

RS - You have listened as I have shared my struggles. You believe in me when I have my doubts. You add so much to all God is teaching me. Thank you.

CT - You read my manuscripts in the roughest of stages and are always positive. Thank you.

KS - If I write it, you read it. You have been a faithful supporter. Thank you.

CT - You asked for it, here it is. I truly hope the words answer your questions.

BK - You listen when I get frustrated, when I am encouraged, and when I just am blah. You always communicate your complete confidence in me. Thank you.

I am very thankful to the Lord for equipping me to write this book. It was a wonderful journey to study God's word while writing this book. I know my God so much better. May you too be blessed.

INTRODUCTION

"For since the creation of the world *God's* invisible attributes, *God's* eternal power and divine nature, have been clearly seen, being understood through what has been made, so that they are without excuse."
Romans 1:20

Any discussion of God needs to begin with the fact that God does exist. Romans 1:20 explains how we can know this truth. The verse is basically an apologetic (systematic argument to defend a position of thought) for the existence of God. The Apostle Paul, the author, argues that God can be clearly seen in what has been made. In other words, our world itself testifies to the existence of God.

Numerous apologetics are used to defend the existence of God. Defending the existence of God, however, is not the same as proving God's existence. Scientifically, in the technical sense of how we measure our world, the existence of God cannot be proven or disproven. God cannot be measured as we measure the physical world.

We cannot physically see God as we see the world around us. We cannot put God under a microscope. We cannot take a measurement tape to God. God is outside our ability to measure. That does not mean God does not exist. It just means God does not exist as we do.

We can say the same about wind. We cannot physically see it. We can see its impact, but we cannot see it. We do not know where it comes from or where it goes. We cannot put it under a microscope. Yet, we still know it exists by the effect we can see and feel. We see the trees move. We can feel our skin respond. Ultimately, it is the impact of the wind on our lives that causes us to believe in it.

Romans 1:20 affirms that we can know God exists by the impact God has on our world. God's attributes, eternal power and nature are seen in our world. The verse says that they are clearly seen. God can be known.

Not just our world testifies of God's existence. God has spoken to us with words. There is God's written word, the Bible, which tells the story of God's relationship with man. Moreover, there is God's living word, Jesus Christ, through Whom man may have a relationship with God.

God can also be known by studying God's impact in the lives of people. God has had a tremendous impact on my life. The challenge is that studying people is not the best mirror of God. For some people, men are the very reason they do not believe in God.

God is God, however, and is not a man. In the chapters that follow, it is hoped that the reader will grow in their understanding and appreciation of who God is. God is a very personal God.

This book discusses God and, in the process, how God is different from man. The only begotten Son of God, the person of Jesus Christ who became man, and the significance of His being born into our world will be introduced. It is through Jesus Christ that God has chosen to have a relationship with us and be known by us.

The lives of biblical characters who suffered evil at the hands of men will be shared. In spite of their pain, these biblical characters were still able to trust and worship God. They had personal relationships with God. We will look at the personal qualities of God that were part of those relationships and are a part of our own relationships with God.

The focus of the book is to know God as God. The use of the male pronoun for God will be avoided so it does not get in the way of knowing God better. Romans 1:20 actually uses the male pronoun for God. The pronoun was replaced with an italicized '*God*.' As you read verses in this book, if you see italicized words within verses, you know that the male pronoun is being replaced. This change was adopted until the final chapters.

It is important that we allow ourselves to know God as God wants to be known. Taking time to know God is the most important decision a person can make. Where do we begin our search to know God? We begin where God begins the story.

CHAPTER 1

THE BEGINNING

"In the beginning God created the heavens and the earth. And the earth was formless and void, and darkness was over the surface of the deep; and the Spirit of God was moving over the surface of the waters. Then God said, 'Let there be...'"
Genesis 1:1-3

We celebrate beginnings. First days of life. First days of school. First days of college. First days of work. First days of marriage. First days of retirement. There is not a first day of God to celebrate.

The Bible, God's story, does not open with the beginning of God. The Bible opens with our first day. Genesis 1:1 opens with 'in the beginning God created.' God said, "let there be" and there was. In addition, while God was creating, we read these celebratory words,

"...and God saw that it was good."
Genesis 1:10, 12, 18, 21, 25

> "And God saw all that He made, and behold, it
> was very good..."
> Genesis 1:31

The Bible opens with God celebrating the creation of the world and man. It pleased God to create our world. It pleased God to create us. God is the beginning and end of all things we know.

While our birth is the opening to the Bible, we are not the most important characters. God is the main character. The Bible is about God's continued relationship with man. The Old Testament (OT) describes God's standard which man could not keep. The New Testament (NT) offers God's solution through Jesus Christ for man's inadequacy. The OT tells the story of God's relationship with man and specifically, with the nation of Israel. The NT tells the story of Jesus, the Son of God, and His church.

God was first. Man came second. The Apostle John recorded these words of God,

> "'I am the Alpha and the Omega,' says the Lord
> God, 'who is and who was and who is to come,
> the Almighty.'"
> Revelation 1:8

Alpha is the first letter of the Greek alphabet and Omega the last. God is first and last. God is the beginning and the end. God is today, yesterday, and tomorrow. God lives forever. The Psalmist wrote concerning man,

> "…And he should cease trying forever – That he should live on eternally; That he should not undergo decay. For he sees that even wise men die; The stupid and the senseless alike perish, And leave their wealth to others."
> Psalm 49:8-10

Man will not live on forever in this world. We will all die one day. Yet, while our bodies do perish, God does tell us that we will exist spiritually. In Jesus Christ, there is provision for an eternal relationship with God (Appendix A). Apart from Jesus, one has an eternity without a relationship with God.

The Apostle John opens his gospel with these words,

> "In the beginning was the Word, and the Word was with God, and the Word was God."
> John 1:1

The true beginning is God. God's Word created us. God's Word, Jesus Christ, recreates us. What does Genesis 1:1 say again, "In the beginning God." God does not exist because of us. We exist because of God. God is God, God is not a man.

CHAPTER 2

GOD IS GOD

"And God said to Moses, 'I AM WHO I AM'; and God said, 'Thus you shall say to the sons of Israel 'I AM has sent me to you.' And God, furthermore, said to Moses, 'Thus you shall say to the sons of Israel…the God of your fathers, the God of Abraham, the God of Isaac, and the God of Jacob, has sent me to you.' This is My name forever and this is My memorial- name to all generations."
Exodus 3:14, 15

To begin to know God, we need to accept that God is who God is. Exodus 3:14, 15 opens with God saying, 'I AM WHO I AM.' It is a wonderful statement of God's certainty of who God is. God did not feel the need to explain any further.

God said these words to Moses as Moses prepared to return to Egypt. God was sending Moses back to Egypt to lead the enslaved nation of Israel away. Egypt was a country with one of the strongest armies of the day. Moses was to demand that the Pharaoh (King) of Egypt let God's people go. Moses would only have his brother Aaron to go with him. Moses is not a king. He is not a warrior. He has no visible army. He just carries a big rod. (If you have not read the story in Exodus 1-14, consider doing so. It is an amazing story of God acting on behalf of God's people.)

From man's vantage point, Moses' situation looked pretty silly and quite dismal. The Pharaoh's name evoked fear. His name carried the power of life and death over his servants. Moses with his brother was to demand that the Pharaoh let a nation of slaves just leave. Two men with a stick are challenging the leader of one of the mightiest armies of that day. It would appear as if power was on Pharaoh's side. Or, was it?

Appearances are not always what they seem. Moses served the King of Kings. God's name evokes God's power. God carries the ultimate power over the life and death of people. Moses was acting in the power of God's name. Moses was acting in the power of God and God's army. The battle was not about who Moses was, but about who God is.

Moses needed God to be God. He needed to know that God is the same yesterday, today and tomorrow. God's trustworthiness is based on the fact that God does not change. The steadfastness of Moses' hope was God's faithfulness. He needed to know that God would do what God said. He needed to know that God is faithful. The only power of hope Moses had was that God is God. He found God true.

God must be who God is, if we are to have faith in times of difficulty. If God is not, what are we to believe? Fortunately, God is faithful to who God is and we can believe in all that God has said. God is who God is forever. Like Moses, we can trust God. We can have assurance that God can and will accomplish what God has said.

God's faithfulness is emphasized in Exodus 3:14, 15 with the words, "the God of your fathers, the God of Abraham, the God of Isaac, and the God of Jacob." God has been the same God from the beginning. The God that Abraham, Isaac and Jacob knew (some 400 plus years prior to Moses) is the same God Moses knew and we can know. God is the same God for eternity. God is the only true God. God is who God has always been and always will be. We can trust in the faithfulness of God's character.

This trustworthiness is further seen in Exodus 3:14, 15 with the statement, "This is My name forever and this is My memorial-name to all generations." God's name can be trusted forever.

Man may change in how they worship God. Man may change in how they communicate with God. Man may change in how they perceive God. God, however, is the same forever. God is known as God is always known. These verses empower our confidence in our God being the same God to all generations. God is who God is. God is not a man that God would change.

The Bible provides the description of the God we are to believe in, if we can just believe. Ah, so simple, just believe, and yet so hard. Believing requires faith in the God that God is and not the god we want God to be.

People say that they cannot believe in God because God does not meet their definition of a loving god. They cannot believe in God because there is evil in the world. They cannot believe in God because people go to hell. There are many reasons for why people say they cannot believe in God. Yet, have they taken the time to know God?

How should we get to know God? Should we ask God to fit who we want God to be? Or, should we just let God be who God is? Should we ask God to change so God is acceptable to us?   Or, should we accept God as God is?

God has provided many ways for us to know God. We can know God through our created world, God's written Word, the Bible, and God's living Word, Jesus Christ. We can know God as God wants to be known. The question one must ask is, "Do I want to know God?"

You will find God, if it is God you seek. However, if you are seeking a god that suits you, then a god that suits you, you will find. And, it will not be the "I am who I am" God. Hear what God says,

"And you will seek Me and find Me, when you
search for Me with all your heart."
Jeremiah 29:13

"And I say to you, ask, and it shall be given to you;
seek, and you shall find; knock, and it shall be
opened to you."
Luke 11:9

You can know God as God wants to be known. God
will meet you in your seeking and answer you. God is God
and will not change. God is not a man.

<u>CHAPTER 3</u>

GOD IS NOT A MAN
PART 1

"God is not a man, that *God* Should lie, Nor a son
of man, that *God* should repent; Has *God* said, and
will *God* not do it? Or has *God* spoken, and will
God not make it good?"
Numbers 23:19

Numbers 23:19 was the verse that came to mind as a
friend shared the difficulty she had in believing in the
Christian God, because God was a man. Men in her life
had been abusive. God being a man was a problem for her
believing in God. She described how many of her friends
struggle with this same issue.

I shared this verse and explained how God being
presented in the male form did not make God a man. God
wants to be known by us and yes, God has chosen a male

gender for communication. Being male, however, does not make God a man. Just as being male does not make a dog a man. God is God.

We discussed this for quite some time. To be honest, I understood her struggle. God's" maleness," at times, has interfered with me getting to know God better. Men have not always been good examples in the lives of many.

While the Bible does portray God as a male, God is not modelled after men. When you consider Numbers 23:19, the Bible is very clear on this subject. The verse rightly begins with 'God is not a man.' The verse continues to explain how God is not like us. Men change. God does not. Men repent. God does not need to. Men do not always do what they say they will do. God always does what God says God will do. God can always be trusted, while men can be untrustworthy.

The use of a pronoun does not define who God is. It only makes it easier for us in referring to God. God's actions and words define who God is. Numbers 23:19 tells us that God's actions and words are the very reason we know that God is not a man. The Apostle Paul wrote to his disciple, Timothy,

> "If we are faithless, *God* remains faithful, for *God*
> cannot deny *who God is*."
> 2 Timothy 2:13

Paul was reassuring Timothy that God can only be who God is. For God to be anything else would be for God to deny who God is. The standard by which we should measure God is by God's standard. What did Paul say? 'God is faithful.'

So, when did we stop measuring God by God's standard? I think it began shortly after our beginning (Genesis 1-3). The whole reason Adam and Eve, first born of mankind, ate the forbidden fruit in the garden was to be more like God. They wanted to be more than who they were. They failed. They became less. I believe the desire to be more like God is still within us and so we make God like us since we cannot be more like God. God did not change that fateful day. We did.

In talking with my friend, she definitely had a problem with having a relationship with God because of the abuse of men. I do not believe she blamed God for the abuse. Other people with whom I have spoken do blame God. Some see God's maleness is one more way men try to dominate. Somehow making God less male makes God safer. A male god is not a good god. Blaming God's maleness becomes a reason for our unbelief.

Surprisingly, it makes sense that we find a way to blame God. We have been doing it since our first disobedience. When Adam was confronted with man's sin in the garden, hear what he said,

> "And the man said, 'The woman whom Thou
> gavest to be with me, she gave me from the tree,
> and I ate.'"
> Genesis 3:12

Adam basically told God that it was not his fault that he ate the fruit God forbid. It was God's fault. God created Eve who gave him the fruit to eat. If God had not created this other person, well, Adam would not have eaten the fruit. Never mind that Adam was present the whole time Eve and the serpent were having the conversation (Genesis 3:1-7). Never mind that Adam knew God's commandment (Genesis 2:16. 17). Never mind that Adam had a choice. It was God's fault.

Evil toward others is a choice we make. Evil others show toward us is their choice. Yet, the tendency is to blame God. Moreover, when men do the evil, how much more is a male god to blame.

People have suffered much pain at the hands of men. Understandably, since God is presented as male, it creates a resistance to believe in God. We do not want God to be a 'man.' While we may understand that God is not a man, the male pronoun can present problems for some of us. It can affect our ability to know God.

Numbers 23:19 is a nice reminder that "God is not a man…nor a son of man." God is God. And, as 2 Timothy 2:13 tells us, God can be trusted to be God, because God cannot deny being God. God can deny being a man.

CHAPTER 4

GOD IS NOT A MAN
PART 2

"So Samuel said to him, 'The Lord has torn the
kingdom of Israel from you today, and has given it
to your neighbor who is better than you. And also
the Glory of Israel will not lie or change…; for
God is not a man, that *God* should change…'"
1 Samuel 15:28, 29

The prophet Samuel spoke these words of judgment to
King Saul after Saul chose to do things his way. King Saul
disobeyed a direct order given him by God. Samuel is
letting King Saul, and us, know that God's decision is final
because "God is not a man."   The standard of measure
used by Samuel was that "the Glory of Israel will not lie or
change."

God is going to do exactly what God said. There will be no changing God's judgment. King Saul cannot exert influence over God as he could over men.

Samuel knew that Saul would want to change God's mind. Saul would want to take the approach with God that he would take with a man. Samuel wants Saul to understand God is not like men. God is not swayed as men are swayed. What God has said, God will do. In fact, it is already done. Notice that Samuel said, "has given." Saul had no control over the choice God had made. Saul cannot manipulate God.

Saul should have known the God of Israel. He was taught in Whom he was to believe. He had been to the temple where they worshipped God and offered up sacrifices. He knew Whom the God was that Samuel was speaking of. Yet, we see that he falls short of knowing God for who God is. Samuel was helping Saul understand who God is. God is not like men whose choices we can change. God is in complete control.

Did faith in God come down to an issue of control for Saul? Does it come down to an issue of control for us? Why do we struggle with letting God be God? Do we want a god we can manipulate? Do we want a god who answers to us rather than God Whom we answer to? Do we want a god who stays away until we want something?

Samuel makes it clear that God is not like us. God is God. God will not be controlled by us. God will not be manipulated by us. God does not answer to us. He actually said to Saul that God is not like men that God 'should change.' God has no reason to change. God is who God is. God was not created by man or for man. Rather, God created man. Genesis chapters 1 and 2 tell us of our creation.

> "And God created man in *God's* own image, in the image of God *God* created him; male and female *God* created them."
> Genesis 1:27

The Hebrew word for man in Genesis 1:27 means mankind. The verse provides its own definition of mankind by saying "male and female He created them." There is a generic sense to the word. "Man" does not mean male, but male and female. This same Hebrew word also appears in Numbers 23:19 in the statement "nor a son of man." There is a second Hebrew word for man in Numbers 23:19 in the statement "God is not a man." While these Hebrew words are different, they both mean mankind in a generic sense.

This usage of two Hebrew words for man in Numbers 23:19 is basically saying that God is neither man nor woman and God is not the son of a man or woman. Man did not give birth to God. God existed before man. The birth of Jesus, the Son of God, was God choosing to be born of flesh to save us. It was not the beginning of Jesus' existence as God, but the beginning of Jesus' existence as man. God was first. God has always existed. There is no beginning to God. Man came second. Man has a beginning.

In fact, Genesis 1:27 tells us that God created Adam and Eve "in *God's* own image." In addition, since God created Adam and Eve, God also created us. What does it mean that 'in the image of God' they were created? Does that mean God is like us? Or, does it mean we are like God? Since we are the created being, we need to consider how we are like God. We describe how a child is like the parent, not the other way around.

The word "image" can mean many different qualities. My mom had blue eyes. None of us kids do. My mom was 5 feet, 2 inches tall. All of us kids are taller. She had two daughters and three boys. Okay, at least two of us were the same sex. All of us kids bare a resemblance to mom, yet none of us are an exact representation of mom. Bearing her image is not the same as being her.

Bearing God's image is not the same as being God. Bearing God's image is not the same as saying God is like us. Exodus 20:1-6 forbids the making of any idol from images in the skies or on the earth or in the water. We are an image on the earth. Exodus seems to say we are not to make an image of God in our image. Our image is not an exact representation of God. God is not like us.

The task, then, is to determine what images we bore at our creation. God is all powerful; we are not. God is all knowing; we are not. God is present everywhere; we are not. God is without sin; He has committed no evil. Adam and Eve were created without sin. Wow, one way Adam and Eve were like God is that they were without sin in their creation. What happened?

Adam and Eve sinned. Adam and Eve ate of the fruit of the tree of good and evil (Genesis 2:1-7), which was forbidden by God. They ate because they thought they would become like God. Instead, they forfeited part of the image they shared with God. They lost their sinlessness. Their act was sin against God. Moreover, that choice cost us our sinlessness as their heirs.

Adam and Eve did not become more like God when they ate of the fruit. God did not become like Adam and Eve. Instead, man became less like God. Adam and Eve lost the sinlessness we shared with God.

God created us in God's image. God was never like us. God is God. As 1 Samuel 15:28, 29 says, 'the glory of Israel will not lie or change…; for *God* is not a man, that *God* should change."

The amazing thing is that God become man in the person of Jesus Christ. Jesus did that for us. Jesus did not stop being God when He became man. Instead, Jesus proved God's faithfulness to man.

CHAPTER 5

JESUS CHRIST GOD AS MAN

"The beginning of the gospel of Jesus Christ, the
Son of God."
Mark 1:1

The best evidence for God being God and not a man is
Jesus Christ, the Son of Man. In Jesus, God became man,
suffered at the hands of men, was resurrected from the
dead, and forgave us. A man could not do that. A man
would not do that.

Jesus must be included in any discussion about who
God is. He is the only way we can know God. He is the
Son of God and He is God. Yes, He became flesh (Son of
Man). Yet, He always was and always will be God. The
Christian faith rests on the Godhead of Jesus Christ. Either
He is who He said He is or He is not. Either he told the

truth or He lied. Moreover, if He told the truth, then He is God.

Jesus' confessed before the Jewish leaders that He was God. It was all they needed to condemn Him to death.

> "…Again the high priest was questioning Him,
> and saying to Him, 'Are You the Christ, the Son of
> the Blessed One?' And Jesus said, 'I am; and you
> shall see the Son of Man sitting at the right hand
> of Power, and coming with the clouds of heaven.'
> And tearing his clothes, the high priest said, 'What
> further need do we have of witnesses? You have
> heard the blasphemy; how does it seem to you?'
> And they all condemned Him to be deserving of
> death"
> Mark 14:61-64

Jesus said two striking things in His answer. First, He said, 'I am.' God's answer to Moses was, "I am who I am." The Jewish leaders heard that. Secondly, He quoted prophecy concerning Himself from Psalm 110 ("the Son of Man sitting at the right hand of Power)) and the book of Daniel ("coming with the clouds of heaven"). The Jewish leaders understood the claim Jesus was making. Jesus claimed to be God. For the Jewish leaders that was blasphemy.

The author of Hebrews writes,

> "God, after *God* spoke long ago to the fathers in
> the prophets in many portions and in many ways,
> in these last days has spoken to us in *God's* Son,
> whom *God* appointed heir of all things, through
> whom also *God* made the world. And *Jesus* is the

> radiance of *God's* glory and the exact
> representation of *God's* nature, and upholds all
> things by the word of *God's* power…"
> Hebrews 1:1-3

These verses tell us many things about Jesus:

1. He is the Son of God.
2. He is the heir of God.
3. Creation is a direct result of Jesus. God created. Since Jesus was involved, He is God.
4. He radiates the glory of God.
5. He is the exact depiction of the nature of God. Jesus is "the exact representation' of God's image."

Who Jesus is, is precisely who God is. When we know Jesus, we know God. The Apostle John in his gospel calls Jesus the only begotten God (John 1:18). Jesus was begotten when He became man. Yet, He was still God. The Apostle Paul wrote that while Jesus knew He was God, He did not exalt Himself (Philippians 2:6). In other letters, Paul wrote that Jesus is the image of God (2 Corinthians 4:4, Colossians 1:15).

Jesus in word and deed confirmed that He was God. He performed miracles only God could perform. His healing miracles confirmed that He could forgive sin. The Jewish leaders knew that only God could forgive sin.

Do you want to know God? You must come to know Jesus as God. Jesus said,

> "I and *God* are one."
> John 10:30

Christ, however, did not come to perform miracles or establish that He was God. He came to save us from our sin. Man needed a savior to have a relationship with God. Man needed a substitute sacrifice for his sins. Jesus Christ is the sin sacrifice.

CHAPTER 6

JESUS CHRIST
SIN SACRIFICE

"And the Lord God commanded the man, saying,
'From any tree of the garden you may eat freely;
but from the tree of the knowledge of good and
evil you shall not eat, for in the day that you eat
from it you shall surely die.'"
Genesis 2:16, 17

To understand the need for man to have a sin sacrifice, which really means a savior, requires understanding the penalty for disobeying God ("you shall surely die"). Adam and Eve disobeyed when they ate from the 'tree of the knowledge of good and evil' (Genesis 3:6). This act of disobedience severed man's relationship with God. Man spiritually died as foretold in Genesis 2:16, 17. Also, as a result of eating the fruit, man is now a sinner. Being sinners gets in the way of us knowing God. Genesis 3:8 describes what happened after they ate the fruit,

> "And they heard the sound of the Lord God
> walking in the garden in the cool of the day, and
> the man and his wife hid themselves from the
> presence of the Lord God among the trees of the
> garden."
> Genesis 3:8

Adam and Eve were not playing hide and seek with God. They did not want to be seen by God. They did not want their nakedness seen by God. It was not only nakedness of body they were hiding. It was also nakedness of soul. They had disobeyed/sinned and they felt exposed. They no longer shared the sinless image with God. They wanted to hide from the holy God who created them. Their sin killed the special relationship they had with God. We inherited this dead relationship from them. Our inheritance as children of God was lost.

Our inheritance is not all that was lost. Man does not just have a problem in his relationship to God. Man also has a problem in his relationship with himself and others. Genesis tells us that they were also aware of each other's nakedness (Genesis 3:7). They covered themselves with fig leaves. Man's innocence was lost.

Nakedness is such a descriptive condition. Is not what most of us desire and fear most is to be completely known? To be completely seen? To be completely accepted and loved? To have to hide nothing about ourselves? To safely expose ourselves to others? But alas, it is not what we know in our relationship with God and each other. Sin is the problem. Sin kills relationships. The Apostle Paul wrote,

> "For the wages of sin is death…"
> Romans 6:23

Romans 6:23 affirms what God declared in Genesis 2:17 when God made it clear that they would die. Death is the only satisfying wage for sin. Good works cannot pay the wages. Good works accomplish nothing in regards to our sin.

The Apostle Paul also tells us:

> "And you were dead in your trespasses and sins,"
> Ephesians 2:1

Ephesians 2:1 is emphasizing that we are already dead. Wait. We are already dead and yet, there is a wage of death to be paid. And, to be quite honest, I feel very much alive. How is this possible? The Apostle is describing the relationship we have with God as a result of sin. While we are physically alive, we are spiritually dead. Our relationship with God died when Adam and Eve ate the fruit.

If we are dead in sin, then have not the wages for sin been paid? If we wish to stay dead, yes. This is why Christ is a sin sacrifice. We can stay dead in our sins or accept Christ's death as payment for our sins. A redeemer (one who pays the price) is needed to restore our inheritance as children of God. Jesus offered up His life as a redeemer to release us from the sentence of death.

Only a relative who is without sin could redeem us. Only a relative who has not sinned could pay the penalty for our sins on our behalf. When Christ became man, he became our relative. He was without sin. He was not subject to the wages of sin. He could pay the price to redeem us. And, pay the price, He did.

The Apostle Paul finishes Romans 6:23 ("For the wages of sin is death") with the following words,

> "…but the free gift of God is eternal life in Christ
> Jesus our Lord."
> Romans 6:23

Paul also wrote in Ephesians,

> "But God, being rich in mercy, because of His
> great love with which He loved us, even when we
> were dead in our transgressions, made us alive
> together with Christ (by grace you have been
> saved),"
> Ephesians 2:4, 5

The Apostle Paul wants us to understand that life is in Christ Jesus our Lord. A living relationship with God is through Jesus Christ. How did Christ do it? If death is required for sin, then how does Jesus coming in the form of man redeem us?   How did He pay the price? He died on the cross for us. Christ died so we could live. His death fulfilled the penalty for our sins.

> "And she will bear a Son; and you shall call His name Jesus, for it is He who will save His people from their sins."
> Matthew 1:21

Jesus became man to pay the wages for our sin. It is a very surreal truth. God chose to be humble and take on the form of man. God became human to save 'people from their sins." Jesus did it to save you and me from our sins. He did it so we could know God. We could not save ourselves from sin; we were already dead. A substitute death was required. Christ was that substitute death.

We can stay dead in our sins or accept that Christ died as our substitute that we might live. Christ died that we could know God in the gardens of our lives. He redeemed what we had in the garden before sin. He restored our inheritance as children of God. He restored the image of God we bore at our creation. God loves us so much that Jesus willingly died. This is who God is.

Accepting that Christ died for us involves an understanding that Christ was without sin and became sin on our behalf. The Apostle Paul wrote to the Corinthian churches,

"*God* made Him who knew no sin to be sin on our
behalf, that we might become the righteousness of
God in Him."
2 Corinthians 5:21

The Him is Jesus Christ. Was Jesus really without sin?
How is that possible since He was born of a woman?

CHAPTER 7

JESUS CHRIST WITHOUT SIN

"You shall not sacrifice to the Lord your God an
ox or a sheep which has a blemish or any defect,
for that is a detestable thing to the Lord your
God."
Deuteronomy 17:1

God required the best of the flock. Sacrifices had to
perfect. Sin is a blemish. For Jesus' sacrifice of Himself to
satisfy God, He had to be without the blemish or defect of
sin. Jesus being without sin is foundational to His ability to
redeem us from sin.

Yet, we have said that all men are sinners. Jesus was a
man. So, how was Jesus without sin? The answer is that
He did not have an earthly father. The Apostle Paul wrote,

"Therefore, just as through one man sin entered
into the world, and death through sin, and so
death spread to all men, because all sinned-"
Romans 5:12

This verse is the most quoted verse to emphasize that sin and the penalty for sin actually passes from the father to the child (Adam is the one man). That does not mean women are without sin. It just means that woman do not at conception pass on the problem of sin to the children. I purposefully said at conception, because the sins of both the mother and father do impact the development of the child.

In the Apostle Paul's letter to the Corinthian churches, he makes it very clear who the one man is through whom sin entered into the world.

"For as in Adam all die…"
1 Corinthians 15:22

Note that is does not say Adam and Eve. It is in Adam that we are conceived in a state of spiritual separation from God due to sin. In Adam we all die. We bear the mark of Adam's sin, and thus his new nature after eating the fruit, to sin. We are born in a state of sin because of Adam.

While Jesus' earthly parents, Joseph and Mary, can be traced back to Adam, Joseph was not Jesus' true father. The Apostle Matthew in his gospel recorded the following words from God to Joseph,

> "…behold, an angel of the Lord appeared to him
> in a dream, saying, 'Joseph, son of David, do not
> be afraid to take Mary as your wife; for that which
> has been conceived in her is of the Holy Spirit."
> Matthew 1:20

Jesus was born without Adam's sin because He was not a child of Adam. He was a child of God through the Holy Spirit. God is sinless, so God's son would be sinless.

Jesus was not only born without sin, He also never committed sin. The writer of the book of Hebrews tells us,

> "For we do not have a high priest who cannot
> sympathize with our weaknesses, but one who has
> been tempted in all things as we are, yet without
> sin."
> Hebrews 4:15

The Hebrews author is comparing Jesus as our high priest to the high priests of the Jewish religion. In Jewish religion, the high priest on the Day of Atonement would make sacrifice for the sins of the people as well as his own sin. Christ made a sacrifice for our sins as our high priest. His sacrifice was Himself. Because He was without sin, His sacrifice of Himself fully satisfied God's requirement for the penalty of sin. No more sacrifices were needed.

Jesus became flesh, so that sin in the flesh could be condemned. So, God's wrath toward sin could be satisfied. His physical death condemned sin. His death on behalf of our sinful flesh delivers us from condemnation. Jesus was spiritually alive, so He could spiritually die for us. By Jesus experiencing spiritual death for us, we can experience spiritual life in Him. Christ said these words on the cross,

> "…My God, My God, why hast Thou forsaken
> me?"
> Matthew 27:46

With these words, we know when Christ became sin and experienced death for us (was separated from His God). Christ suffered our spiritual death. He paid the ultimate price. After these words, Jesus "yielded up His spirit" (Matthew 27:50) and "the veil of the temple was torn in two" (Matthew 27:51).

Within the Jewish temple (church) was the holy place and the most holy place. A veil separated the two. While priests daily served the Lord in the holy place, the high priest could only enter the most holy place once a year. It was forbidden for anyone else to enter. The high priest entered once a year to make atonement for sin. Death awaited him if he did not approach God in the right way. When Christ died, this veil was torn in two.

The veil symbolized man's inability to enter the most holy place in God's temple. The tearing of it signaled that there was now nothing to separate us from our God. In Christ, we can enter the Holy of Holies where God is. Christ, who was without sin, was the perfect male sacrifice to atone for our sins.

Was it necessary that Jesus be a man? Yes, because God required male sacrifices.

CHAPTER 8

JESUS CHRIST
MALE SACRIFICE

"And Isaac spoke to Abraham his father and said,
'My father!' And he said, 'Here I am, my son.'
And he said, 'Behold, the fire and the wood, but
where is the lamb for the burnt offering?' And
Abraham said, 'God will provide for Himself the
lamb for the burnt offering, my son.' So the two
of them walked on together…Then Abraham
raised his eyes and looked, and behold, behind him
a ram caught in the thicket by this horns; and
Abraham went and took the ram, and offered him
up for a burnt offering in the place of his son."
Genesis 22:7-13

Abraham had been asked by God to offer up his son as
a sacrifice to God. He needed God to provide a substitute

sacrifice to save his son's life. We need a sin substitute sacrifice to save our lives. We need a sinless relative to pay the wages for our sins. Does this sacrifice require a male substitute? Yes. As early as Genesis 22, God desired male sacrifices ("a ram caught in the thicket").

Genesis 22:1-14 tells the story of Abraham preparing to offer up his son, Isaac. It was through Abraham, and later Isaac, that God promised to bless the nations. These verses describe how God supplied a substitute sacrifice so that Isaac might live. God provided a male animal, a ram, as the substitute sacrifice.

The New Testament describes how God provided the substitute sin sacrifice for us that we might live. Jesus Christ is the substitute sacrifice for man's sin. Jesus is a male substitute. God provides male substitutes. A male lamb for Isaac. Jesus Christ, a male lamb (John 1:29), for us.

In the Old Testament, there are numerous examples of God desiring a male sacrifice. Exodus 12:1-30 is the inauguration of the Passover ceremony for the Israeli nation. The nation at the time was enslaved in Egypt. There was a total of 10 plagues brought upon the nation of Egypt before freeing the Israeli nation. The Israeli nation left shortly after the completion of the final plague.

The tenth and final plague was the death of all firstborns in the land. God, however, provided a substitute sacrifice for the Israeli nation so that their firstborns would be passed over and live (the reason for the Jewish Passover ceremony). Without this substitute sacrifice, the firstborn of the Israelites would have died as well.

> "Speak to all the congregation of Israel, saying,
> 'On the tenth of this month they are each one to
> take a lamb for themselves, according to their
> fathers' households, a lamb for each
> household...Your lamb shall be an unblemished
> male a year old; you may take it from the sheep or
> from the goats."
> Exodus 12:3-5

Male lambs were sacrificed to provide blood for the people to spread on the lintel of their homes and doorposts. The blood signified a substitute sacrifice so that the firstborn children of Israel would live. The male lamb's blood was the substitute sacrifice for the plague. The angel of the Lord passed over the homes bearing the blood.

This is metaphorically what will happen on God's final judgment day. Those of us who bear the blood of Christ will be passed over when God passes judgment. Without the sacrifice of Christ's shed blood, people are not spared the judgment of God. God requested a male lamb sacrifice. And yes, God would know the difference.

After the exodus from Egypt, sacrificial offerings were a daily part of Jewish life and religious practice. The Book of Leviticus describes the various offerings. Some offerings required substitute sacrifices. Male sacrifices were dominantly required. Here are a few of those offerings:

> "If his offering is a burnt offering from the herd,
> he shall offer it; a male without defect..."
> Leviticus 1:3

"Now if his offering is a sacrifice of peace offerings, if he is going to offer out of the herd, whether male or female, he shall offer it without defect before *God.*"
Leviticus 3:1

"if the anointed priest sins so as to bring guilt on the people, then let him offer to the *God* a bull without defect as a sin offering…"
Leviticus 4:3

"Now if the whole congregation of Israel commits error…and they commit any of the things which the *God* has commanded not to be done, and they become guilty; when the sin which they have committed becomes known, then the assembly shall offer a bull…"
Leviticus 4:13-14

"When a leader sins and unintentionally does any one of all the things which *God* has commanded not to be done, and he becomes guilty, if his sin which he has committed is made known to him, he shall bring for his offering a goat, a male without defect."
Leviticus 4:22-23

> "Now if anyone of the common people sins
> unintentionally in doing any of the things which
> the Lord has commanded not to be done, and
> becomes guilty, if his sin, which he has committed
> is made known to him, then he shall bring for his
> offering a goat, a female without defect..."
> Leviticus 4:27-28

A male animal was to be the sacrifice except for two offerings. A female animal could be sacrificed for peace offerings and for sin offerings for a person not in a position of leadership. In the case of the peace offering, the animal could be either male or female.

A final offering for consideration is on the Day of Atonement. The Day of Atonement was for the cleansing of all the sins of the nation of Israel. It is described in Exodus 16:1-28,

> "And he shall take from the congregation of the
> sons of Israel two male goats for a sin offering and
> one ram for a burnt offering."
> Leviticus 16:5

Not surprisingly, male animals were offered for the atonement of sin. A male sacrifice to pay the penalty for man's sin was the requirement. Jesus became man to fulfill this demand. He came to sacrifice Himself on our behalf. He came to make atonement for our sin. The Apostle John wrote these words of John the Baptist (whose ministry prepared the people for the coming of Jesus),

"The next day he saw Jesus coming to him, and
said, 'Behold, the Lamb of God who takes away
the sin of the world!'"
John 1:29

Jesus is referred to as the "Lamb of God." Now, we understand why. Jesus Christ was the male lamb sacrifice God required. Christ became man for the sole reason to be sacrificed for the atonement of our sins. His death was the substitute penalty for our sin.

It is humbling to ponder Christ's sacrificial death. God became man to die for us. Christ died so we could again enjoy our inheritance as children of God. He died that we would again know life in our relationship with God. He died so that we might live with God forever. Is there a greater love? I think not. The Apostle John wrote,

"Greater love has no one than this, that one lay
down his life for his friends."
John 15:13

Christ laid down His life for us. Jesus Christ is the center of any conversation about God. Jesus is God and not a man. Yes, He chose to become a man during a point in our history to save us from our sin. Yet, He is, always has been, and always will be God.

"Jesus Christ is the same yesterday and today, yes
and forever."
Hebrews 13:8

While in Christ we are saved from our sin, we still live in a sinful world. We are still impacted by our own sin and the sin of others. There is suffering in our lives. How do we believe in God in the midst of the suffering? There are biblical lives that were able to believe in the midst of their suffering. Suffering is not new. They suffered and still believed. They knew God.

CHAPTER 9

KING DAVID SUFFERED LOSS

"I have become estranged from my brothers, And
an alien to my mother's sons."
Psalm 69:8

Often when we tell the stories of King David, we leave out the suffering of loss. We tell the story of Goliath, stories of victorious battles, his writing of the Psalms and his time as king. Yet, David suffered much loss in his life. He was estranged from his family, his wife, his country, and his home. He lived among his enemy. His closest, faithful friends were outcasts of his country. He was homeless for much of his young life. As a Jew, his life had become unacceptable according to the faith of his fathers. In many ways, he was alone.

His brothers burned with anger against him, the king whom he faithfully served wanted him dead, and while he sacrificially fought the enemies of the Israeli nation, he was considered a traitor. He humbled himself to his enemy that he might provide for his family. I am not sure his life could get any worse because of men.

Yet, through it all, he loved God. He had faith in God. He faithfully served God. He wrote beautiful songs (Psalms) to the Lord. When given the opportunity to kill his enemy, King Saul, he did not. David would be king with the death of Saul. David, however, waited. Yes, there were advantages to killing Saul. Yet, God's honor was more important to David.

David was living in caves and was a wanderer with no home. He did not have a safe place to rest his head. He worked without wages. He had no man to turn to for help. Yet, he did have God. David did not let the mistreatment of men interfere with his knowledge of God.

His story begins in 1 Samuel:

"So Samuel did what the Lord said, and came to Bethlehem…And he said, 'In peace; I have come to sacrifice to the Lord. Consecrate yourselves and come with me to the sacrifice.' He also consecrated Jesse and his sons, and invited them to the sacrifice…Thus Jesse made seven of his sons pass before Samuel. But Samuel said to Jesse, 'The Lord has not chosen these.' And Samuel said to Jesse, 'Are these all the children?' And he said, 'There remains yet the youngest, and behold, he is

tending the sheep.' Then Samuel said to Jesse,
'Send and bring him; for we will not sit down until
he comes here.'"
1 Samuel 16:4-11

These verses almost read like a male Cinderella. Jesse knew the significance of Samuel's coming and did not have his youngest son, David, home. Surely, God would choose one of his other sons. No, God had chosen David. Just as the glass slipper would only fit on Cinderella's foot, the king's crown would only fit on his head.

To provide a little history, Israel had a king, King Saul. However, he disobeyed God and so God was giving the kingdom to another. David was the other. David did not ask for this honor. God bestowed it.

Shortly after this encounter with Samuel, David finds himself serving as King Saul's armor boy (1 Samuel 16:21). He was on leave from his duties to Saul when the nation is confronted with the challenges of Goliath (1 Samuel 17). Hear the attitude of his brothers when David approaches the battlefield,

"Now Eliab his oldest brother heard when he
spoke to the men; and Eliab's anger burned against
David…"
1 Samuel 17:28

His "anger burned against David". He was not just angry. He was enraged. It was a searing, burning fire of anger. This is not an enemy of David's; this is his brother who should have love for him. David was estranged from those whom he should have been closest to.

David defeats Goliath and soon finds he now has an enemy in King Saul and must flee. He has few supporters of his countrymen and thus, must rely on the friendships and loyalties of other nationalities. He was an outcast among his people. He lived in the wilderness. He lived as a criminal though he had done nothing wrong. Here is a young man that Samuel consecrated as the next king of Israel who was a homeless wanderer surviving through the kindness of others who were considered outsiders by his religion.

David was a young man who lost his family, his home and his country. He lost it because of the evil of others. Others that he served and loved. What did David do to deserve this? It appears that his mere existence was the problem.

David, however, faithfully served his God in spite of the harm others sought against him. He did not blame God. He did not view God differently because of man's evil treatment. I daresay that was difficult to do.

The Bible does not specifically talk about David's questioning of his life circumstances, but it does tell us of his faithfulness to God. Even when David had a chance to kill King Saul, which would make sense since King Saul was trying to kill him, he did not. David waited on the Lord. David trusted the Lord. David did not make God meet his definition. David did not require God to act according to David's perception. He accepted God's plan.

David does eventually become king according to God's plan. These are God's words concerning David,

> "…I have found David the son of Jesse, a man
> after My heart, who will do all My will."
> Acts 13:22

God said these words when he picked David to be king. He said these things before David had been consecrated by Samuel, before he fought Goliath, before he honored King Saul by not taking his life, before he battled without reward on behalf of the nation of Israel and before he became king. God saw his heart and chose him. While others had evil in their hearts toward David, God had love. God had affection. God had compassion.

God sees your heart. He sees the pain and the brokenness. He also sees the person you were meant to become. He knows the plan He has for you (Jeremiah 29:11).

I do not know what your family situation is like, but God does. I do not know how you have been or are being mistreated by those in authority, but God does. I do not know what kind of life you have lived to date, but God does. God can redeem it all. David could see past the hurts and unfairness of life and believe in God. He could believe in the faithfulness and goodness of God. God was faithful and good to David.

God wants to help you to look past the hurts and know His gracious love. God is not like the evil men and women in our lives. King David knew God's love. Rahab the harlot knew God's love.

CHAPTER 10

RAHAB THE HARLOT WAS ABUSED

"Then Joshua the son of Nun sent two men as
spies secretly from Shittim, saying, 'Go, view the
land, especially Jericho.' So they went and came
into the house of a harlot whose name was Rahab,
and lodged there."
Joshua 2:1

This is an inspiring story. The Israelites are beginning
to take possession of the land promised their ancestors.
They had already won some key battles when they
approached the city of Jericho. Joshua, the leader of the
Israeli nation, sent out spies to investigate the city. Who

does God use to hide the spies and keep them safe? Rahab the harlot.

Here is a woman who has been used by men for one purpose, to satisfy their lusts. Most likely, her beginning as a harlot started by her father selling her to the temple of Ashtaroth to serve as a prostitute. Jericho was a city in Canaan that worshipped Ashtaroth, the goddess of the moon.

The worship typically entailed men giving to the temple coffers in exchange for time with a temple prostitute. Upon completion of their service to the temple, the women were left to fend for themselves. Rahab only knew one way to make money. She continued in the selling of her body.

Think about what 'her' god asked of her. Now, the nation of Israel enters her story with a more powerful God. What might a more powerful God ask of her? Amazingly, rather than have disdain for this greater God, she sought Him out.

Imagine the abuse she experienced as part of the worship of her country's lesser god. Surely, she should have feared the abuse of this greater God. She did not. Her beautiful words are recorded in Joshua 2:9-13. Here is part of verse 11,

> "…for the Lord your God, He is God in heaven
> above and on earth beneath."
> Joshua 2:11

She had heard of the acts of God on behalf of the Israeli nation. She knew of the kings that had already been defeated. She knew her city would fall as well. She believed that the God of Israel must be the true God. Rather than reject God, she asked for kindness,

> "Now therefore, please swear to me by the Lord,
> since I have dealt kindly with you, that you also
> will deal kindly with my father's household…"
> Joshua 2:12

Rahab believed she would find kindness from this greater God. What amazing faith. She was not raised to believe in the God of Israel. She had only heard the stories of God's deliverance of the Israeli nation and the battles won. She only knew of how her god and men used her to meet their needs. And, here she was trusting God. Her faith was rewarded.

Ironically, she did not just ask for kindness for herself, but for her family. The same family that abandoned her to a life of prostitution. No, we do not know the whole story. Yet, Rahab probably had good reason not to care about her family and definitely not to believe in God. Yet, she did care and she did believe.

Rahab and her family were spared. They are the only people of Jericho spared. And while they joined the Israelites, initially they had to stay outside the camp (Joshua 6:23). Rahab and her family were unclean gentiles by Jewish teaching. Yes, they were alive. Yet, they were outcasts. She was a harlot.

Her story continues in the New Testament in the book of Matthew,

"The book of the genealogy of Jesus Christ…and
to Salmon was born Boaz by Rahab; and to Boaz
was born Obed by Ruth; and to Obed, Jesse; and
to Jesse was born David the king…and to Jacob
was born Joseph the husband of Mary, by whom
was born Jesus, who is called Christ."
Matthew 1:1-16

This harlot is listed in the lineage of Jesus. This
daughter of God, who started as an outcast to the nation of
Israel, is listed in Jesus' family tree. Yes, Rahab found
kindness. She also found salvation in the Lord. To God,
she was a daughter that God loved. She was a daughter for
whom God cared.

She was honored by God. Hebrews 11 is the Hall of
Faith for Old Testament believers. Only two women are
mentioned; Rahab is one of those women.

God is not ashamed of her. God is not ashamed of her
past. God did not treat her as men did. God accepted her
and gave her a name above so many others. God redeemed
her. He gave her a new life in Him.

I think if Rahab was with us today, she would say,
"Trust God, my sons and daughters. God's love is greater
than any love you will ever know. God will tenderly care
for you and shelter you. God is not like men. God is God.
God was my salvation. God rescued me. God gave me a
new life. God will give you a new life. You can trust God."

Maybe you can identify with Rahab. Maybe you can
identify with the abuse. God washed her clean. God is

proud to be called her God. God did not hide her past but embraced it. God embraced Rahab. She was a daughter whom God loved with a whole heart. God honored her as a member of Jesus' family tree and in the Hall of Faith. God is not like men. He does not seek people to use, but people to save.

Can you let God see you? Can you let God embrace your past and love you? Can you let yourself trust God? Rahab could. Joseph could.

CHAPTER 11

JOSEPH SECOND TO PHAROAH WAS ABANDONED

"…So Joseph went after his brothers and found them at Dothan. When they saw him from a distance and before he came close to them, they plotted against him to put him to death."
Genesis 37:17, 18

Joseph is a young 17 years old in Genesis 37. His brothers, by his father's other wives, want him dead. Actually, they want to kill him. So much for family love.

It is one thing to not get along with family; it is another for them to plot to kill you.

The brothers would have killed him except one brother, Reuben, thought better of it. Joseph was placed in a pit until his brothers could decide what to do with him. This pit was actually a well whose water supply had dried up, so it was quite deep.   Imagine being put in a pit from which you cannot climb out. You are in this pit waiting to know what further harm is to be inflicted upon you. Would you feel abandoned?

His brothers did not kill him, but instead sold Joseph into slavery. His brothers had such hatred and resentment toward Joseph that they could so easily betray him. He was abandoned by people he trusted. What sense of loss.

Joseph became a slave in a wealthy man's home in Egypt. He performed well in his new home and quickly became the highest ranking slave, if there is any comfort in that. Joseph served his owner with loyalty and honor. The betrayal by his brothers did not keep Joseph from being honorable in his treatment of others. His master knew that God was blessing him because of Joseph.

Well, it is not just his owner that desired Joseph's labors. His master's wife also took an interest in him. Her interest, however, was not moral. She wanted Joseph to serve her in her bedroom. She wanted to use Joseph to satisfy her physical desires. Joseph had a choice. Joseph chose to obey God. The same God that allowed him to become a slave.

Joseph chose God's way and found himself in prison. Wait a minute. This less than honorable woman tried to seduce him, he resisted, and now he was in jail? Yes. The master believed his wife concerning Joseph's intention and Joseph was now in prison. Biblical characters endured hardship at the hands of men. They endured betrayal and abandonment at the hands of men.

While in prison, Joseph again rose to prominence. The chief jailer put him in charge of all other prisoners. He, too, recognized God's blessings. Joseph's attitude of service does say a lot about his faith in God.

He is joined in prison by the Pharaoh's chief baker and cupbearer. He interprets their dreams for them. In three days, they will be before the Pharaoh. One will live and one will die. Joseph asks the cupbearer, who will live, to please do him a kindness by helping him to get out of prison. He said he would help Joseph, yet, He forgot about him for two years. The Bible emphasizes that it was 'two full years' (Genesis 41:1). Joseph was again abandoned by one whom he served.

What is it about Joseph that such evil was committed against him? The Bible tells us that his brothers did not like his special relationship with their father. The slave master's wife did not like that he would not lie with her. She probably was not used to being turned down. The cupbearer seemed to lack any appreciation.

Does your life ever feel like Joseph's? Do people seem to make your life situations worse? Do people you thought you could trust do you harm or forget you? For all the good you do, is life getting worse rather than better? Do you feel unappreciated by those in your life?

Joseph faithfully served those two years in prison until the opportunity to be set free finally presented itself. The

Pharaoh had a dream no one could interpret. Yes, the cupbearer remembers Joseph now. He is brought to Pharaoh to interpret the dream. He interprets it and,

> "So Pharaoh said to Joseph, 'Since God has
> informed you of all this, there is no one so
> discerning and wise as you are. You shall be over
> my house, and according to your command all my
> people shall do homage; only in the throne I will
> be greater than you."
> Genesis 41:39, 40

Joseph's life just took a significant turn. Joseph now served the Pharaoh. Think of the new power Joseph had. He was the second most powerful person in Egypt. Joseph has the power to seek revenge. There was the slave master and his wife that led to several years in prison. There was the cupbearer who forgot him for two years. Joseph, however, did not seek revenge. We understand why when he again sees his brothers.

Pharaoh's dream had to do with seven years of abundant crops followed by seven years of famine. During the famine, only Egypt had the grain people needed. Even Joseph's family needed to turn to Egypt for subsistence. Eventually, the brothers are face to face with Joseph. Upon learning whom Joseph was, his brothers feared his retaliation. Instead, Joseph replied,

> "And now do not be grieved or angry with
> yourselves, because you sold me here; for God

> sent me before you to preserve life…And God
> sent me before you to preserve for you a remnant
> in the earth, and to keep you alive by a great
> deliverance. Now, therefore, it was not you who
> sent me here, but God…"
> Genesis 45:5-8

Even as I write this, I am humbled my Joseph's attitude. He accepted the evil of his brothers as God's will for his life. That is faith. He did not blame God. He claimed that God worked it toward the good of his family. He could accept the abandonment and trust God.

When we evaluate his life, we see that being a slave and a prisoner prepared him to serve the Pharaoh during this crisis. As a slave, he learned to manage another man's property for his profit. He learned to serve. As a prisoner, he learned to manage desperate people in a desperate situation. The famine was making people desperate. I can understand what God was doing in his life. I can appreciate how he was preparing Joseph. I am still humbled by Joseph's faith. He did not let the evil intentions of men interfere in his trust of God.

Interestingly enough, after their father died the brothers were fearful that Joseph might now act in causing them harm. I guess they too had found his attitude astounding. They came to him to plea for mercy for themselves. Joseph graciously responded,

> "…Do not be afraid, for am I in God's place?
> And as for you, you meant evil against me, but

God meant it for good in order to bring about this
present result, to preserve many people alive."
Genesis 50:19, 20

What a profound statement by Joseph. Yes, his
brothers meant evil. God had a plan. God meant it for
good. Perhaps people have committed evil against you.
God has a plan.

Joseph was able to give the circumstances of his life to
God. God used those circumstances to do great things in
Joseph's life. When the Israeli nation finally leaves Egypt,
Joseph's bones go with them. The bones of his brothers
did not. God honored Joseph in life and in death. God
wants to honor you.

Joseph was able to separate the acts of people from
God. He understood that God was not like men. God is
God. Queen Esther understood that as well.

<u>CHAPTER 12</u>

QUEEN ESTHER DID NOT BELONG

"Now there was a Jew in Susa the capital whose
name was Mordecai…And he was bringing up
Hadassah, that is Esther, his uncle's daughter, for
she had neither father nor mother…"
Esther 2:5-7

Esther was an orphan. She lived during the time of
Israeli exile under Persian rule. She was raised by a male
cousin, Mordecai. We do not know the circumstances of
her family and why it was a cousin and not an aunt or
grandparent. We do know she was an orphan. We can
assume she was raised in a single parent home. She lived in
another's home in another's country. She did not belong.

Her becoming queen was hastened by the disobedience
of another queen. During the occasion of a party given by

the King (Esther 1), the King wanted his Queen Vashti to model her beauty to the men in attendance. It was not just a matter of being present to be seen. He wanted his queen to display her naked body to a room full of men so they could gaze upon her. She refused. Rather than have her killed, he had her banned.

Desirous of a new queen, all the beautiful young virgins in the kingdom were gathered. One would become his queen. Esther found herself, a young Jewish virgin girl, in the household of the king to serve at the pleasure of the king. He would have sex with her without marriage. Her consent was not necessary. He may or may not make her queen. Her life would never be her own. She did not belong.

She was selected queen, yet her Jewish heritage was kept a secret. Among the king's staff was a man, Haman, who despised the Jews and especially hated Mordecai, Esther's cousin. The stage was now set. You had the Jewish queen in one corner and the king's trusted servant who hated Jews in the other.

Haman was able to get the king to issue an edict that on a specific day all Jews were to be killed. Jews were not allowed to own weapons and so, were in no position to defend themselves. Mordecai approached Queen Esther and basically told her to plead to the king on behalf of her people.

What Mordecai was requesting of Esther was significant. For good reason, Esther was afraid to do what Mordecai asked. Here is how approaching the king worked:

"All the king's servants and the people of the
king's provinces know that for any man or woman
who comes to the king to the inner court who is
not summoned, he has but one law, that he be put
to death, unless the king holds out to him the
golden scepter so that he may live. And I have not
been summoned to come to the king for these
thirty days."
Esther 4:11

Esther could be facing death to approach the king. On top of that, the king had not shown any interest in her presence for the last thirty days. Mordecai challenged her reluctance and she requested prayer. She knew she would need God's protection to approach the king.

Why would she believe God would protect her? He took her parents. He did not protect her from being taken into the king's house. God had not protected the Jews, including her, by allowing Haman's edict to be issued. Yet, it was God she would need to trust. She would need God's protection.

When Queen Esther approached the king, he extended the scepter. Queen Esther was able to get a new edict issued that allowed the Jews to defend themselves. It was a complete reversal of events. Esther was able to let God be God, in spite of her circumstances. God was able to use Esther mightily. She could have bemoaned all the times God seemed to fail in protecting her, but she did not. She trusted God to be God. Life's circumstances were life's circumstances.

I am not saying it was easy for her. She fasted for three days and asked others to do the same before she approached the king. She knew the risk. She knew God might not deliver her. She also knew it was in God whom she trusted. She believed in God's plan for her life.

I have learned a lot from Esther's approach to life. Her life was not free of pain and suffering. She lost her parents. She was raised in a single parent home. She had to serve at the whim of a king. She was in a marriage that was not based on love. Yet, she was able to endure the circumstances of her life and trust God.

She submitted with grace. She chose to submit. She was not a doormat. She chose to trust God and wait on God. She did not try to take matters into her own hands, but she sought God. She suffered hardship. She suffered loss. She found God faithful.

Visitors can see the alleged Tomb of Esther and Mordecai in present day Hamadan, Iran. The tomb of these two Jews is an historical place in the Islamic country of Iran. God honors His children.

Esther understood that God is God; God is not a man. She, like other biblical characters, knew the God in Whom she believed. The key word is knew. She knew God. She knew she belonged as a child of God.

God wants to be known by us. God wants to meet that need of belongingness in us. God desires for us to take a close look at who God is. God has revealed to us how God can be known. God has presented qualities of God's nature in the Bible that we might know God as these biblical characters knew God.

CHAPTER 13

GOD'S QUALITIES

"But the fruit of the Spirit is love, joy, peace, patience, kindness, goodness, faithfulness, gentleness, self-control; against such things there is no law."
Galatians 5:22, 23

In seeking to know who God is, there are several approaches to consider. Typically, the attributes of God are discussed. Attributes such as all powerful and all knowing. Many a book is written about these attributes. When thinking about how we bear God's image, it seems fitting to discuss God's qualities as found in Galatians 5:22, 23. These verses actually call the qualities "the fruit of the Spirit." The Spirit being the Spirit of God.

Studying this fruit is appropriate, since Jesus said to His disciples,

"I am the vine, you are the branches; he who
abides in Me, and I in him, he bears much fruit;
for apart from Me you can do nothing."
John 15:5

The fruit of a vine describes the vine. It is the vine that bears the fruit. Christ is the vine. Thus, the fruit the vine bears describes who Christ is. Moreover, if it describes Christ, it describes God.

This concept of the vine and its fruit helps me. I do not really know one tree or vine from another. A tree is a tree. A vine is a vine. However, if I see the fruit, I can tell you what kind of tree or vine it is. If there are cherries, it is a cherry tree. If there are grapes, it is a grape vine. If Jesus is the vine, we can know God by the fruit of the vine. The fruit of the Spirit tells us what kind of vine God is.

The challenge is that we cannot see God and Jesus is no longer with us in the flesh. How do we see this fruit of the Spirit by which we can know God? That is where the life of Jesus as recorded in the Bible helps. Jesus Christ spoke the words in John 15:5. Jesus also said,

"If you had known Me, you would have known
My *God* also; from now on you know *God*, and
have seen *God*…He who has seen Me has seen
God…"
John 14:7-9

As we know Jesus, we know God. If we want to know God, we need to study Jesus. As we study the fruit of the

Spirit over the next several chapters, we will be studying Jesus. Jesus is the vine. It is His fruit. It is God's fruit. Interestingly enough, the first fruit listed is love.

CHAPTER 14

GOD IS LOVE

"But God demonstrates *God's* own love toward us,
in that while we were yet sinners, Christ died for
us."
Romans 5:8

I am glad the first fruit stated in Galatians 5:22, 23 is love. Everything God does starts with God's love toward us. This verse clearly states that "God demonstrates" love toward us. God's love is active. So active, that Christ died on the cross that we might know the greatness of God's love. The Apostle Paul wrote:

"But in all these things we overwhelmingly
conquer through *God* who loved us. For I am
convinced that neither death, nor life, nor angels,
nor principalities, nor things present, nor things to
come, nor powers, nor height, nor depth, nor any

other created thing, shall be able to separate us
from the love of God, which is in Christ Jesus our
Lord."
Romans 8:37-39

In addition, Jesus said:

"Greater love has no one than this, that one lay
down his life for his friends."
John 15:13

God's love is proven in Jesus Christ. Christ laid down
His life for us. Nothing can separate us from that love.
That is not a human love. That is God love. God's love is
real. God's love made the ultimate sacrifice.

This is how the Apostle Paul described love:

"Love is patient, love is kind, and is not jealous;
love does not brag and is not arrogant, does not
act unbecomingly; it does not seek its own, is not
provoked, does not take into account a wrong
suffered, does not rejoice in unrighteousness, but
rejoices with the truth; bears all things, believes all
things, hopes all things, endures all things. Love
never fails… "
1 Corinthians 13:4-8

I want someone to love me as Paul describes. God does
love me so. God does love you so. God actually loves us

so much more. It is this demonstration of love that separates the faith of Christians from all other religions.

A defining demonstration of God's love toward biblical characters that I so appreciate is God's love toward Adam and Eve after they sinned. It is a very tender moment of love. Adam and Eve upon eating the forbidden fruit immediately knew that they were naked and clothed themselves with fig leaves. The writer of Genesis tells us what God lovingly did:

> "And the Lord God made garments of skin for
> Adam and his wife, and clothed them."
> Genesis 3:21

God showed love toward Adam and Eve with this first sacrifice of an animal to provide clothing for them. An animal was killed so Adam and Eve could adequately be clothed. Yes, God passed judgment (Genesis 3:8-24) for their sin. God also demonstrated tender love in covering their nakedness.

Often, I think what we desire most is for someone to see our nakedness and then cover it with love. God did that for Adam and Eve. God wants to do that for us. God wants to cover our nakedness of sin with the blood of Christ. He wants to clothe us in Christ's sacrificial death.

Man has done many evil things in the name of love. God has not and cannot. While we fear what God could do with the power God has, God cannot act outside of who God is. Remember how Paul told Timothy that God cannot deny who God is (2 Timothy 2:13). God is also holy and cannot perform evil. God's love is bound by God's holiness.

While holiness is not listed as a fruit of the spirit, it is a God quality. God is not a man. God is a holy God who loves us. The Apostle John wrote:

> "In this is love, not that we loved God, but that
> *God* loves us and sent *Jesus* to be the propitiation
> for our sins."
> 1 John 4:10

As can be seen by the many verses shared, Christ is the ultimate expression of God's love for us. Christ was brutally beaten, then suffered on the cross, before dying for our sins. Not only did Christ suffer physically for the forgiveness of our sins, He suffered spiritual death for the penalty for our sins.

I often wonder if the reason we struggle with God's love is because we do not fully grasp the damage of choosing our way over God's way. Choosing our way wholly separates us from God.

Only God's work, as a result of love, demonstrated by the life, death and resurrection of Christ can repair the damage of our choices of doing things our way. Out of love, God has chosen to repair the damage through Christ. God chooses to have a relationship with us.

Do we want a relationship with God? Are we ready to give up our ways so we can know God's love toward us? Are we willing to submit to God's way for our lives? What would it mean for us to allow God to see our nakedness and clothe us in love? What would it mean to have a relationship with God on His terms? God's terms are faith in the sacrificial death of Jesus Christ. God's way is to love us and give us joy.

CHAPTER 15

GOD IS JOY

"fixing our eyes on Jesus, the author and perfecter
of faith, who for the joy set before Him endured
the cross, despising the shame, and has sat down at
the right hand of the throne of God."
Hebrews 12:2

It is appropriate that the fruit of love is followed by the fruit of joy. When you watch new love, joy is the description of the lovers' countenance. The love of another gives us joy.

Joy is the word the author of Hebrews used to describe what Jesus felt about enduring the cross for our sins. When I contemplate what emotions I imagine Christ feeling concerning the suffering He would endure on the cross, joy is not on my list. How could Christ experience joy?

What about suffering such pain could possibly give Christ joy? What about dying such a brutal death on the cross could possibly give Christ joy? What about being separated from His Heavenly Father could even come close to giving Christ joy? His love for us. His joy was focused on what He would accomplish.

His joy was in our salvation. Our relationship with God being restored was His joy. It was our eternal life with God that gave Christ joy to endure the humiliation, pain and brutality of the cross. It was my forgiveness of sins and your forgiveness of sins that gave Christ joy. It deserves our contemplation that Christ's death on the cross was an act of God's joy. The Apostle Paul tells us:

"For the wages of sin is death, but the free gift of
God is eternal life in Christ Jesus our Lord."
Romans 6:23

God freely gives us eternal life in Christ and it gives God joy to do so. I wish there was a way in writing to pause and have you meditate on the fact that your relationship with God is the joy for which Christ endured the cross. I cannot think of anyone in my life who has so joyfully suffered for me; but Christ did. This is profound.

Christ joyfully suffering for me definitely did not fit my early definition of who God was. I thought God was a stern judge waiting to punish me for sin. Instead, God takes joy in forgiving me. God wants to demonstrate love toward me by forgiving me. It gives God joy. This is a God I want to know. This is a God worth knowing. If that was not enough, hear what Jesus said,

"These things I have spoken to you, that My joy
may be in you, and that your joy may be made
full."
John 15:11
And,

"Until now you have asked for nothing in My
name; ask, and you will receive, that your joy may
be made full."
John 16:24

Jesus is telling us that God wants us to have joy and for it to "be made full." When you think of something being full, it cannot hold anything else. God wants us to have so much joy, that there is not room for anything else. Think of your happiest moment and that does not compare with the joy God wants you to have. The joy God wants us to have is completely satisfying. God wants us to have the kind of joy Jesus knew so that He could go to the cross. That is powerful joy.

John 16:24 continues this thought by saying to us that the reason God answers our prayers is so that our joy is full. We want the answer to our prayer and God wants to answer to give us joy. Ironically, we are thinking of ourselves and God is thinking of us. The joy of the Lord is sweet.

Christ endured the cross for the joy of our salvation. Christ wants that joy to fill us. We are the joy of God and God wants to be our joy. The reality of our joy is due to the peace we have with God through Christ.

CHAPTER 16

GOD IS PEACE

"Peace I leave with you; My peace I give to you;
not as the world gives, do I give to you. Let not
your heart be troubled, nor let it be fearful."
John 14:27

When we understand God's love and joy, it follows that we will have peace. It is not just any peace, however, just as it is not any love or joy. Christ tells us, in John 14:27, that He will give us His peace. He also tells us that it is not the peace "the world gives."

What does all that mean? What peace is Christ giving us? Then, He adds, 'Let not your heart be troubled, nor let it be fearful.' This verse is rich. Is Christ saying that the peace He will give us will calm our troubled hearts and give us courage in the midst of our fear? What is this peace we will have?

It is the peace Christ had just before He prayed in the Garden of Gethsemane, was betrayed, suffered and died on the cross. He is eating His last supper with the disciples when He spoke these words of giving them peace.

He is preparing His disciples for what awaits Him this evening and the following day. He knows that they will be troubled and afraid. He wants them to have His peace. He is at peace.

As we review Christ's final hours in the Garden of Gethsemane (Matthew 26:36-42), we gain an appreciation of the depth of His emotions, and more specifically His peace, concerning the coming of His suffering and death on the cross. Here is what He said to His disciples:

"Then He said to them, 'My soul is deeply grieved,
to the point of death; remain here and keep watch
with Me.'"
Matthew 26:38

Christ's soul was 'deeply grieved.' Yet, He had peace and gave His disciples peace. He wanted them to have His peace. I marvel that it is peace and not strength or faith or love or power or…He felt it was His peace they would need most for the difficult times that awaited them. What is the significance of His peace?

If we look at His life, it definitely was not peace with man. Men wanted Him crucified and did crucify Him. It was not world peace because He did not even talk about that. That leaves one peace. Christ's peace was peace with God, our Creator.   In spite of what lay ahead of Him,

Christ had peace with God. He knew God was in control and had a plan.

He told them it was a peace that the world could not give. I chuckle a bit with these words, because I have never felt peace in the world. I am trying to understand what kind of peace the world could give. I do know the kind of peace we talk about in the world; we talk about the absence of war. The absence of war, however, is not peace. Just because men do not war, does not mean they are at peace with one another.

Jesus was at peace with God. Jesus was at peace with Himself. Jesus was at peace with His enemies. Here are His Words as he hung on the cross,

> "But Jesus was saying, 'Father, forgive them; for
> they do not know what they are doing...'"
> Luke 23:34

Christ extended forgiveness toward those who crucified Him. He definitely had peace. He had peace that went beyond man's definition. The dictionary defines peace as a period of time of harmony between people. Christ's peace was not a period of time. It was a state of being for Him. He wants it to be a state of being for us.

Maybe God's peace is hard for us because it is a state of being. It is peace with God. It is peace with self. It is peace with life's circumstances. Jesus was at peace.

Interestingly enough, Jesus never had a period of time of harmony with His enemies. His enemies were always seeking an opportunity to discredit Him and eventually kill

Him. Yet, He had peace. He wants us to have that same peace. Christ's words to His disciples after speaking of His peace were

"You heard that I said to you, 'I go away…' "
John 14:28

The reason the disciples would be troubled is because Christ said He was leaving. They have followed Him, slept under the stars with Him, and have experienced His power in a mighty way. What are they supposed to do when He leaves? They left families and jobs to follow Him and He said He is going away. How could He leave them after they left everything to follow Him? Yes, they were troubled.

Christ told them not to be troubled. He is telling us not to be troubled. Christ told them not to have fear. He knows the cross awaits Him and knows the disciples will be afraid. What does Christ do? He gives them His peace.

Christ was not troubled. Christ was not afraid. He had peace with the will of God. He wanted His disciples to have peace with the will of God. God wants us to have the same peace. Christ came, died and was resurrected that we might have peace.

The Apostle Paul describes God's peace this way,

"And the peace of God, which surpasses all comprehension, shall guard your hearts and your minds in Christ Jesus."
Philippians 4:7

Christ's peace will protect our troubled hearts. His peace will guard us in our fears. His peace surpasses anything we have ever known. His peace is enough. Peace with God is what the soul seeks. The souls of men and women find rest in His peace. Peace gives us patience.

CHAPTER 17

GOD IS PATIENCE

"The Lord is not slow about *God's* promise, as
some count slowness, but is patient toward you,
not wishing for any to perish but for all to come to
repentance."
2 Peter 3:9

The Apostle Peter comes right out and tells us that God is patient because God does not want any to perish. God wants people to come to repentance and know the love, joy, and peace that can be known in Jesus Christ. It is a calming thought to think God is patient with us. God is patient with sinners.

One of the best examples in scripture of God's patience toward sinners is found in the Old Testament. God had promised Abraham and his descendants the land of Canaan, however, it would not happen immediately. God explained to   Abraham, in   Genesis 15: 13-16, that his descendants would not inherit the Promised Land for hundreds of years.

> "And God said to Abram, 'Know for certain that your descendants will be strangers in a land that is not theirs, where they will be enslaved and oppressed four hundred years. But I will also judge the nation whom they will serve; and afterward they will come out with many possessions. And as for you, you shall go you fathers in peace; you shall be buried at a good old age. Then in the fourth generation they shall return here, for the iniquity of the Amorite is not yet complete.'"
> Genesis 15:13-16

Abraham's descendants, the chosen ones of God, would spend 400 years as slaves because the sin "of the Amorite is not yet complete." Isn't it fascinating that God was patient toward the Amorite, a people that was not included in the promise to Abraham? He has made a promise to Abraham and yet, the fulfillment of the promise must wait because of God's patience toward the Amorite. The Amorite were the current occupants of the land God promised Abraham. God's explanation for the patience was that their sin was not complete. God's patience was not because of a promise God made the Amorite. God's patience was because God is patient.

Abraham's descendants would take possession of the land after God's patience was satisfied. It was actually 430 years before it was satisfied. There is such rich conversation to have around this, yet for this discussion, the focus is God's patience. God waited. And because God waited, Abraham's descendants waited.

Some translations use the term long-suffering rather than patient. I would say God waiting hundreds of years to punish the Amorite for their sin was long-suffering.

When considering the word long-suffering; it gives a depth to God's patience. Imagine painful endurance of someone who is difficult to be around for a long period of time. Actually, even a short period of time with some people can require painful endurance. Can you think of people in your life who are painful to be around? Does it feel like suffering?

We are those kind of people for God. We disrespect God. We are rarely happy with God. We blame God when things go wrong. We do not want to worship God when things are going well. We do not want to know God as God wants to be known. We demand that God meet our definition. We ask and ask of God, yet get upset when God asks of us. God provides a solution for our sin, Christ, and we reject Christ. We basically throw temper tantrums when life does not go our way. We can act like spoiled brats.

God is long-suffering toward us. God is not quick to punish us. God was not quick to punish the Amorite. God wants us to come to repentance. God wants us to know forgiveness. One day, God will pronounce judgment as God did with the Amorite. Today, God patiently waits.

I think of the saying, "Patience is a virtue." We usually hear it or say it when we are not very patient. Waiting is hard for us. Fifteen minutes is the classic acceptable wait time for someone if we have a choice. We leave as fast as we can, after that "long" wait time. God's timeframe for the Amorite was four generations. God's patience toward us is our lifetime.

Have you ever considered how patient God is toward you? God is long-suffering, because that is who God is. God is patient, because God does not wish for you to perish. God is the very essence of patience. He patiently waits to show us kindness.

CHAPTER 18

GOD IS KINDNESS

"Or do you think lightly of the riches of *God's* kindness and forbearance and patience, not knowing that the kindness of God leads you to repentance?"
Romans 2:4

God's kindness has a purpose. God's kindness leads us to repentance. God's kindness is directly related to God's forbearance and patience.

Repentance is a recognition that we deserve God's judgment; that we are guilty of sin against God. It involves a changed heart in regards to our ability to save ourselves. Repentance leads us to Jesus.

God's forbearance is God's patient endurance; God abstaining from the enforcement of a right.   God's right is to judge us. Instead, as the Romans 2:4 is telling us, God through kindness is patiently abstaining from doing what

God has a right to do in hopes that we will have a changed heart.

God has told us "the wages of sin is death" (Romans 6:23). The judgment of God is that we can die in our sins or accept Christ's death for the judgment of our sins. God through kindness leads us to repentance, so we accept by faith Christ's death. Instead of judging us, God forbears with us so God will not have to judge us.

Romans 2:4 is emphasizing that it is with kindness that God leads us to this recognition of guilt to be set free. Men often use shame or punishment or fear of pain to get us to admit guilt. I am sure you can think of other methods. God, however, is not a man. God uses kindness.

God does not want to judge us. God wants to save us from the judgment for our sin. God's love is the motivation and kindness is the way it is communicated. God acts with kindness toward us.

Acts of kindness can heal so many hurts. One person who is kind to us can change our whole outlook for our day and even our lives. The Apostle Paul, in Romans 2:4, calls the acts of God's kindness, riches. We are rich in God's acts of kindness. What a beautiful thought. Here is what the psalmist had to say,

> 'Many, O Lord my God, are the wonders which
> Thou hast done, And Thy thoughts toward us;
> There is none to compare with Thee; If I would
> declare and speak of them, They would be too
> numerous to count.'
> Psalm 40:5

The psalmist is overwhelmed with God's kind acts and thoughts toward him. The kindness of God led the psalmist to God. It leads us to God. God's kindness does not lead to the judgment of God; it does not lead to the commandments of God. The kindness of God leads us to the love, joy and peace we have with God through Christ

God is kind toward us with patience. As I ponder the long-suffering of God's kindness, I think of these words of Jesus:

"You have heard that it was said, 'You shall love your neighbor, and hate your enemy.' But I say to you, love your enemies, and pray for those who persecute you in order that you may be sons of your *God* who is in heaven; for *God* causes *God's* sun to rise on the evil and the good, and sends rain on the righteous and the unrighteous. For if you love those who love you, what reward have you? Do not even the tax-gatherers do the same? And if you greet your brothers only, what do you do more than others? Do not even the Gentiles do the same? Therefore you are to be perfect, as your heavenly *God* is perfect."
Matthew 5:43-48

According to Matthew 5:43-38, how is our God perfect? God is perfect in the kindnesses shown to the unrighteous, as well as, the righteous. The sun rises and rain is provided for both. God does not just bless the one and curse the other. God is kind to both.

The 'religious' people of Jesus' time on earth had many criticisms of Jesus. The striking criticism, when we consider kindness, is that Christ associated with those that the religious found unworthy. Christ associated with those whom were considered the scum of the earth. Christ associated with prostitutes, lepers, and tax gatherers. He showed kindness to people the religious leaders denounced. Christ showed kindness to people like you and me. In response to the criticism, Christ said:

> "…It is not those who are healthy who need a
> physician, but those who are sick; I did not come
> to call the righteous, but sinners."
> Mark 2:17

Christ came to show kindness to those who need kindness. He leads sinners (us) to a relationship with God through kindness. Christ wants sinners to experience the love, joy and peace they have through a relationship with God.

When we look at the many healing miracles performed by Jesus, we see people who were outcast and rejected by men. A person could become an outcast just by touching them, so others would avoid them. Christ did not avoid them. Christ showed kindness toward them. Many of these people had not known personal touch for years. Christ was personally touching them. Christ was kindness.

There are so many examples in scriptures of God's kindness. There is the widow who helped Elijah, the Samaritan woman, King Hezekiah, Lazarus, the thief on the cross, and even the Apostle Paul. The story that means most to me is my own salvation. God has been kind to me.

I give God no reason to love me, to be patient with me, to be kind toward me. Yet, God does all that and more, because of who God is. God's kindness leads me to repentance over and over again. I know God will forgive me and not punish me when I come to him seeking compassion. God will accept me. God will be kind toward me. The Apostle Paul so perfectly stated:

> "But when the kindness of God our Savior and
> *God's* love for mankind appeared, *God* saved us,
> not on the basis of deeds which we have done in
> righteousness, but according to *God's* mercy, by the
> washing of regeneration and renewing by the Holy
> Spirit, whom *God* poured out upon us richly
> through Jesus Christ our Savior, that being
> justified by *God's* grace we might be made heirs
> according to the hope of eternal life."
> Titus 3:4-7

In God's kindness, we find mercy and grace leading to eternal life. Does not this sound like a God you want to know in a more personal way? Does this sound like a God who is good?

CHAPTER 19

GOD IS GOODNESS

"Do not remember the sins of my youth or my transgressions; According to Thy lovingkindness remember Thou me, For Thy goodness' sake, O Lord."
Psalm 25:7

In Psalm 25:7, the psalmist is asking God not to remember his sins or transgressions for the goodness of God. This is an amazing request. This is more than just asking God to be kind toward him. The psalmist is asking God not to remember any harm or disobedience done by him. This request is made solely upon the goodness of God.

What is this request requiring of God? It means God cannot hold a grudge. It means God cannot judge the sin later. It means God cannot bring it up later when the psalmist again fails. In other words, God is not to do what we so often do with each other. God is not to remember our wrong doing ever again.

The psalmist portrays God's goodness as the basis for God not recalling or remembering our sins or transgressions. God's goodness forbids him from doing certain things. While forbidden can be seen as a negative word, we need to understand that God's goodness, like God's holiness, requires certain things of God. Therefore, when God acts with love and kindness, the actions must be consistent with God's holiness and God's goodness. God's goodness does not allow God to remember our sins once forgiven in Christ.

The psalmist is stating that God will not remember his sins because God is good not because the psalmist is good. This is an astounding concept: God forgets my sins because God is good.

I can think of relationships where I wish friends would not keep reminding me of when I blew it or failed or…God does not remember and God does not remind me. God, out of goodness, chooses not to remember. God, out of goodness, cannot remember. My past is truly in the past to appear never again in the present. The next time you are reminded of sin you have confessed and recognized God's forgiveness, please know that it is not God who is reminding you. God has chosen not to remember our sins. Since God does not remember them, God does not remind us of them.

As I reflect on God's goodness, I have to admit that when I thought about describing God through the fruit of the Spirit, I did not anticipate how much I would come to understand God's commitment to us. God's goodness is not just about the forgiveness of our sins, but the forgetting of them. God remembers our sins no more. It is beautiful what the Psalmist asks. The Psalmist is asking God to remember him, yet not remember his sin. In other words, God would know him as he can be fully known without his failures interfering. He can be naked before God as Adam and Eve were before they sinned. He trusts God's goodness to answer his request.

God's goodness reassures us that God can see us apart from our sin. God can look past our sin and see us. Actually, God does not even see our sin; God only sees us. God sees Christ perfected in us; perfected in me and perfected in you. That is goodness. Hear what the Psalmist says:

> "As far as the east is from the west, So far has *God* removed our transgressions from us. Just as a father has compassion on his children, So the Lord has compassion on those who fear *God*. For *God* knows our frame; *God* is mindful that we are but dust."
> Psalm 103:12-14

As I was selecting the above verse, I could not help but think of those who have not had good fathers. When you have a father that is not good and lacks compassion, it is hard to think of God in that way. My heart goes out to you. God's heart goes out to you.

Our earthly fathers are not perfect. They, too, have been damaged by sin. When the damage an earthly father can cause is considered, it is scary to consider the damage God could cause. God's goodness, however, prevents God from damaging those whom God loves. Yes, God will judge the ungodly. However, for those of us who know Christ, we experience God's goodness. God can only act in our best interest.

Somehow, we must let God heal us of the sins of our fathers. We must learn to forgive and see that the kindness of the Lord leads us to repentance. We must learn that the goodness of the Lord separates our sins and their sins from us as far as the east is from the west. The east and the west never meet. Once forgiven, God's goodness assures that our sin is removed from us. It no longer exists. Oh, to experience the sweet, sweet goodness of the Lord.

Psalm 103:14 tells us that God knows our frame. God knows how you have been damaged. God knows your hurts and doubts. God knows your fears. God's goodness fully accepts you. God is ready to fully love you and put the hurts and sins of your past as far from you as the east is from the west.

Bathe in the goodness of God. Let the goodness of God penetrate your heart so you can know the love, joy, peace, patience and kindness of God. Let the goodness of God help you to experience God's faithfulness.

CHAPTER 20

GOD IS FAITHFULNESS

"The Lord's lovingkindnesses indeed never cease,
For *God's* compassions never fail. They are new
every morning; Great is Thy faithfulness."
Lamentations 3:22, 23

The hymnal words, "Great is Thy faithfulness, Great is Thy faithfulness, morning by morning new mercies I see" come to mind.   God's faithfulness confirms that God's qualities of love, joy, peace, patience, kindness and goodness are "new every morning."   God's faithfulness to who God is, is guaranteed.

Isn't it nice knowing that God's wonderful qualities are faithfully new every morning? New means that they have not been affected by the previous day's deeds. New means they never get old; they never wear out. We get tired. God does not tire. God's faithfulness is based on who God is and not on our performance.

Every day is a new day with God. Every day God is ready and waiting to love us. Caring for us and providing for us never gets old for God. God is continually faithful.

I had a boss that as soon as he said good morning I knew what he was going to be like that day. He either was going to be great and supportive. Or, he was going to chew you up and spit you out. It was unnerving. I really liked him on his good days and avoided him like the plague on his bad days. This is not how God is. God is the same every day. God is faithfully loving, joyful, peaceful, patient, kind and good.

This enduring faithfulness of God is difficult for us to grasp. Like my boss, people fail us all the time. One day a person is your friend, and the next day he/she is not. If you have moved around a lot like I have, one minute they know you and the next minute they do not. It was as if as soon as I left town, I ceased to exist. Not so with God.

Faithfully, God is always with me. Every day God shows his love toward me. Every single day I get to experience how great God is. I do not have to wait for the good morning as I did with my boss. God is the same every morning. The psalmist wrote,

"Thou hast enclosed me behind and before, And
laid Thy hand upon me. Such knowledge is too
wonderful for me; It is too high, I cannot attain to
it. Where can I go from Thy Spirit? Or where I
can flee from Thy presence? If I ascend to

heaven, Thou art there; If I made my bed in Sheol, behold, Thou art there. If I take the winds of the dawn, If I dwell in the remotest part of the sea, Even there Thy hand will lead me, And Thy right hand will lay hold of me. If I say, 'Surely the darkness will overwhelm me, And the light around me will be night,' Even the darkness is not dark to Thee, And the night is as bright as the day. Darkness and light are alike to Thee."
Psalm 139:5-12

The psalmist understood God's faithfulness to us. No matter where we find ourselves, no matter what situation in which we find ourselves, God will be with us. God will be faithful to us through the good and bad in life. God is faithfully with us. We are never alone.

These are beautiful verses for meditation. There is nowhere we can go and not find God faithful. There is nothing we can do and not find God faithful. No matter how dark life may seem to get, God will faithfully light the way for us. What did God say to Joshua just before leading the Israeli nation into the Promised Land?

"…just as I have been with Moses, I will be with you; I will not fail you or forsake you."
Joshua 1:5

God's faithfulness did not allow God to fail or forsake Joshua. God's faithfulness does not allow God to fail or forsake us. Listen to what the writer of Hebrews tells us,

> "Let us hold fast the confession of our hope
> without wavering, for *God* who promised is
> faithful;"
> Hebrews 10:23

The Apostle Paul told Timothy,

> "If we are faithless, He remains faithful; for *God*
> cannot deny *God's character.*"
> 2 Timothy 2:13

In addition, we have the Apostle Paul's words to the church in Thessalonica,

> "Faithful is *God* who calls you, and *God* also will
> bring it to pass."
> I Thessalonians 5:24

God's faithfulness does not allow God to be anyone other than God. God's faithfulness is why God's "lovingkindnesses never fail" and God's "compassions never fail." God is faithful.

As we study these verses, it is clear that God's faithfulness is all about who God is. God does not need our faithfulness. God is not because we are; God is because God is and God faithfully is. God will be faithful to you. Every day, God is faithful to God's character toward us. Every day, God is faithful with gentleness.

CHAPTER 21

GOD IS GENTLENESS

"Thou has also given me the shield of Thy
salvation, And Thy right hand upholds me; And
Thy gentleness makes me great."
Psalm 18:35

We have studied many wonderful qualities of God and yet, it is God's gentleness that makes us great. I never associated gentleness with greatness. I never associated God's gentleness as making me great. The psalmist did.

Here are some descriptions of gentleness:

- Does not mean weakness.
- Involves humility and thankfulness toward God.

- Polite, restrained behavior toward others.
- Mild and soft.
- Value and quality of one's character.
- A strong hand with a soft touch.

My favorite description can be summarized as it takes a strong person to be truly gentle. Do we equate gentleness with strength? The psalmist did. His words are, 'Thy gentleness makes me great.'

I also like the description, a strong hand with a soft touch. The psalmist said, 'Thy right hand upholds me.' With a soft touch, God's strong right hand upheld the psalmist and upholds us. God's greatness toward us is found in God's gentleness.

Such simplicity that greatness comes from gentleness. Seems so contrary to the way our world works. It is this contrariness of it that makes it God. Man does not view gentleness as a strength. God does. In the book of Matthew we read,

> "Blessed are the gentle, for they shall inherit the earth."
> Matthew 5:5

Rulers of men do not use gentleness. They use power and might. God's word tells us that gentleness is stronger. Christ came with gentleness. Christ spoke these words,

> "Come to Me, all who are weary and heavy-laden, and I will give you rest. Take My yoke upon you,

and learn from Me, for I am gentle and humble in
heart; and you shall find rest for your souls. For
My yoke is easy, and My load is light."
Matthew 11:28-30

Christ tells us that He is "gentle and humble in heart."
When you consider the power Christ demonstrated with
healings, the casting out of demons, calming storms,
feeding five thousand people with five loaves of bread and
two fishes, is not it ironic that He says He is gentle and
humble? It is as if Christ is saying that His power came
from His gentleness and humility. If we ponder this
concept, we understand that it did. One of the definitions
for gentleness is 'humility and thankfulness toward God.'
Christ submitted His will to God.

Christ could be gentle because He was not weakened by
it, and those He ministered to were strengthened by it. We
are strengthened by God's gentleness. This is so contrary
to way men think. Again, God is God, God is not a man.
In God, we find the love we seek. We find the compassion
we so desperately need. We find the gentleness to
strengthen us.

As we consider opportunities to show gentleness, we
need to be mindful that it is not a weakness but a strength.
We are doing just as our Lord did. Others are strengthened
by our gentleness just as we are strengthened by His. Christ,
in Matthew 11:28-30, encourages us to learn from Him.
And what qualities does he accentuate in His statement?
The two qualities He chose are gentleness and humility.
Probably the two hardest qualities for the natural man.

Jesus teaches us with gentleness and promises that as we trust Him we will bear the fruit of gentleness. We will bear the strength of gentleness. I really feel the need to stress that gentleness is a strength. We are being strongest when we are being gentlest. That is such a beautiful picture of truly loving another. Our God is a gentle God who exercises self-control.

CHAPTER 22

GOD IS SELF-CONTROL

"No one can serve two masters…"
Matthew 6:24

It is appropriate that self-control is the last listed fruit. What makes those other qualities so strikingly perfect in Jesus is His self-control. Jesus was always in control of Himself. Even as He was being crucified, He was in control. We read in Luke,

"And Jesus, crying out with a loud voice, said, "Father, into Thy hands I commit My spirit." And having said this, He breathed His last."
Luke 23:46

Until His very last breath, Jesus was in control. His life was not taken from Him. He offered His life up. He offered His life up for us. Jesus said, "No one can serve two masters." He understood that better than anyone did. His "self-control" was directly related to Whom was His master. God was His master.

The Greek word for self-control is actually from the Greek word for mastery. What a perfect connection with the above verse, Matthew 6:24, which provokes the questions, 'Who is your master?' "Who is in control?"

When I played the flute, I was the master of the instrument for the making of beautiful music. The flute could not make beautiful music on its own. It needed someone who had mastered the art of playing a flute. If you were a flute, who would play you? Would it be a masterful artist or someone else?

There is only one masterful artist for us. God is the masterful artist of the universe and us. Only as our master can God make beautiful music with our lives. Only as our master can God cause the fruit of the Spirit to be who we are. Jesus understood that and lived it as an example for us to know what a loving master God is.

We hate the word master. It carries with it someone who has control of our every move. Yet, when we look at the fruit of the Spirit, it says self-control, not God control. God as our master gives us control. It is a beautiful collaboration. We see this collaboration in the life of Jesus.

Jesus was under the control of the Spirit of God and thus, emoted self-control. At Jesus' baptism, we read from the testimony of John the Baptist,

"And John bore witness saying, 'I have beheld the Spirit descending as a dove out of heaven, and He remained upon Him...'"
John 1:32

The Spirit of God descended upon Jesus. Right after that we are told,

"And immediately the Spirit impelled Him to go out into the wilderness. And He was in the wilderness forty days being tempted by Satan..."
Mark 1:12, 13

Jesus exemplified exercising self-control in the power of the Spirit. The Spirit led Him into the wilderness to be tempted by Satan. Jesus willingly went. Self was under the control of the Spirit. Self was in submission to the Spirit. Self was in submission to God.

Satan tempted Jesus' three times. The third temptation connects with Matthew 6:24 (opening verse for chapter):

"Again the devil took Him to a very high mountain, and showed Him all the kingdoms of the world, and their glory; and he said to Him, 'All these things will I give You, if You fall down and worship me.' Then Jesus said to him, 'Begone, Satan! For it is written, 'You shall worship the Lord your God, and serve Him only.'''
Matthew 4:8-10

When Jesus responded with His words, He was quoting from Deuteronomy 6:13. Just before this quoted verse in Deuteronomy, we read,

"then watch yourself, lest you forget the Lord…"
Deuteronomy 6:12

Jesus' response in Matthew 4:8-10 is clear, serve only one master, "the Lord your God."' Exercise self-control or as Deuteronomy 6:12 says, "watch yourself." We are to submit the control of self to the Spirt of God to "serve God only."

Jesus modelled this kind of self-control. Jesus allowed Himself to be led by the Spirit. Jesus worshipped the Lord our God first. Jesus worshipped God as a man should. Jesus did not have two masters. Jesus said,

"…My food is to do the will of *God* who sent Me,
and to accomplish *God's* work."
John 4:34

Jesus was controlled by the will of God who sent Him. He did not have two masters. We cannot have two masters. We can only love one master. Will our master be God or will our master be another?

This mastering through self-control is so needful for the other fruit to ripen. It is only through the power of the Spirit of God that any of the fruit is possible. The fruit needs to stay attached to the vine for life. When the fruit is separated, it dies. Jesus stayed attached to His relationship with God. We need to stay attached to our relationship with God. There is only one vine that produces the fruit of self-control. Christ is the vine.

It is interesting that at the end of the list of the fruit, we find the words, 'against such things there is no law." Where there is self-control, there is no need for rules. None of us likes rules. The fruit of the Spirit requires no rules.

CHAPTER 23

AGAINST SUCH THINGS THERE IS NO LAW

"For sin shall not be master over you, for you are
not under law, but under grace."
Romans 6:14

We are under grace. We are under grace because of
Jesus who died for us. We are not under law. How
wonderful. God does not seek to put us under a list of laws.
God seeks to give us the life Jesus lived. Jesus lived a life
free to love God and be loved by God. Jesus knew Who
His master was.

The question remains of who will be our master? Romans 6:14 teaches us that sin can be our master. It teaches us that sin puts us under the law.

Sin was not master over Christ. God, His Father, was His master. Jesus knew that any other master led to sin. Ironically, because God was His master, He fulfilled the law for us. Later in Romans, this is what the Apostle Paul wrote concerning Jesus, the law, the Spirit of God, and us

> "For what the Law could not do, weak as it was through the flesh, God did: sending *God's* own Son in the likeness of sinful flesh and as an offering for sin, *God* condemned sin in the flesh, in order that the requirement of the Law might be fulfilled in us, who do not walk according to the flesh, but according to the Spirit."
> Romans 8:3, 4

These few verses summarize the work of the Spirit in producing the fruit of God in us. It fulfills the law of God. Sin does not need to be our master. God can be our master. Only God, through patience and kindness, leads us to such freedom from the law. Jesus by being "an offering for sin" set us free from the law. Sin was condemned and "the requirement of the Law" fulfilled in Christ's death on the cross.

Please understand that Jesus was not condemned for violating any law of God or man. He was condemned, by God, for our violations of God's laws. It was God's plan for setting us free from the law of sin. There was no law against who Jesus was or what Jesus did. Jesus freely submitted to His death. Jesus freely obeyed.

Is not that the freedom we seek? To obey because of who we are not because of a law. I never want to walk on the grass until a sign tells me not to. It is as if the sign takes away my freedom. Signs never took away Christ's freedom.

While Christ was free, He did serve one master. Christ served God, His Father. Christ did not serve under compulsion. He served with joy. It was for the joy of our salvation that He endured. Christ did not need laws to govern His behavior. The law of God was written on His heart. The law of God was enough.

It is the same law that Paul says in Romans 8:3, 4 is fulfilled in us by the Spirit. The bearing of the fruit of the Spirit fulfills the law. When you look at the fruit - love, joy, peace, patience, kindness, goodness, faithfulness, gentleness and self-control - do you see laws? Or, do you see grace?

Would you not rather be under the Spirit and be known for such qualities or trudge through life obeying laws? Christ did obey the laws. His obedience, however, was who He was rather than what He did.

Jesus understood something we struggle with. We struggle with obedience to laws. He knew that giving His life to God was the fulfillment of the law and was life. Jesus knew that knowing God was life. Jesus was God so it did give Him an intimate understanding. An intimate understanding that He wants to share with us. An understanding that sets us free from needing laws to govern our behavior.

In America, we love laws. Politicians work full-time writing new laws. It is actually quite sad that we spend so much time, energy and money writing laws of which most of us are oblivious.

All of us violate some laws of our land without even knowing it. There are just too many laws to keep track of. When I served on a grand jury, the law(s) would be read to us first so we knew what the crime was. The state I lived in required that all criminal cases be presented to Grand Jury before going to trial. We would hear numerous cases every day.

With all the drug cases we heard, I eventually had the laws memorized. It was amazing the minute differences for each law. One law that scared me is that carrying my prescription drugs in anything other than the prescription bottles was considered a crime. I did not know that I was breaking the law by carrying my prescription drugs in a pill carrier. We try to control behavior through laws.

Jesus' behavior was not controlled by laws. Jesus served God, and thus fulfilled the law. The Jewish leaders could not find fault with Him in relation to God's law. The Roman leaders could not find fault with Him in relation to man's laws. Because of His complete submission to God, there were no laws against who He was.

Here is what Jesus considered the most important laws,

"Jesus answered, 'The foremost is, 'Hear, O Israel!
The Lord our God is one Lord; and you shall love
the Lord your God with all your heart, and with all
your soul, and with all your mind, and with all your

strength.' The second is this, 'you shall love your neighbor as yourself." There is no other commandment greater than these."
Mark 12:29-31

This is how Jesus lived His life. He loved God first, and loved us like Himself. Who needs laws with that kind of love? Jesus is love. The fruit of the Spirit is who Jesus is. Jesus is who God is.

Is it not interesting that laws are typically against behavior? Laws tell us what we cannot do. Christ tells us what we can do.

Why do we need so many laws? Why do we need so much direction for our behavior toward one another? It is easy to think we need all these laws because of those few people who do evil. Yet, if there were not laws, and thus consequences for illegal behavior, would we be so good? If we did not get a ticket for running a red light, would we stop at a red light? Sometimes, maybe. All the time, probably not.

We need all these laws because of a lack in us. We lack the power within us. We often want to do the very thing we are not supposed to do; like walk on the grass. We need God. As we bear the fruit of the Spirit, laws are not needed to govern our behavior. It is a beautiful picture.

Jesus needed no laws. Jesus did not lack. He was the perfect man. He allowed us to glimpse the perfection of our God. Jesus healed. Jesus forgave. Jesus cared about the outcasts of society. Jesus cared about the downcast. Jesus cared about the hurting. Jesus cared about people.

Jesus loved. Jesus had only one master. His master was God. He did not need laws. He was free to serve.

I sit here wanting you and me to appreciate the freedom we have when God is our master. We have love, joy, peace, patience, kindness, goodness, faithfulness, gentleness and self-control. We are not under law. We are under grace. We can live life as Jesus lived.

It is a thing of beauty to walk in the power of the Spirit as Jesus did. It is a liberating feeling to be so empowered by the Spirit that we bear the fruit of Christ. It is truly invigorating to know that the all-powerful God is working gently on our behalf. There is no law to hinder the Spirit from working in our lives and on our behalf when we know Christ.

Knowing Christ is so important. To know Christ is to know God. To know God as God wants to be known is to know life as God intended.

CHAPTER 24

KNOWING GOD IN THREE PERSONHOODS

"Go therefore and make disciples of all the
nations, baptizing them in the name of the Father
and the Son and the Holy Spirit."
Matthew 28:19

Up to now, we have discussed God, and more specifically, the Son of God, Jesus Christ. As Matthew 28:19 depicts, God is known by three 'personhoods.' These personhoods represent relationship roles through which God communicates with us. The three personhoods or roles are Father, Son, and Holy Spirit. While we also know God as God, that is not a revelation of personhood but rather, a matter of truth.

As we study the Bible to know God, we learn in the Old Testament (OT) that people knew God as God, Lord and Spirit. God was not referred to as "Father" very often. God was represented in the male gender. The Israelites actually avoided saying the name of God. There was a reverent fear rather than a personal relationship with God as the theme. However, as we look at biblical characters, we see a very personal God. Abraham, Moses and David, to name a few, all had a personal relationship with God.

As Lord, God was the appearance of a man. We read this of Abraham's encounter with the Lord,

"Now the Lord appeared to him…And when he lifted up his eyes and looked, behold, three men were standing opposite him…"
Genesis 18:1, 2

Abraham actually saw three men. The scripture does not tell us who the other two men were. It is clear that the Lord was one of the three. I cannot help wondering if the Lord was Jesus.

The Spirit in the OT was seen in the actions of God in creation and in the gifting of men to perform certain duties. In Exodus 31:3, we read how God work through an artisan for the building of the tabernacle to house the ark of God.

"And I have filled him with the Spirit of God in wisdom, in understanding, in knowledge, and in all kinds of craftsmanship."
Exodus 31:3

While people in the OT were able to have a relationship with God, it was different than in the New Testament (NT). They were under the law and thus, subject to the animal sacrifices for sin. They could not rest in the forgiveness of their sins in Christ's death as we can.

In the NT, these three roles of God in our lives are much more intimate and more personal. We see Jesus, the Son, in the flesh ministering to people. He is referred to as Lord. Jesus introduces us to the intimate way God is our Father. We are children of God.

Jesus gives us the Holy Spirit. The Spirit of God is always present in believers in Jesus rather than just present when a particular job requires God's help. Jesus called the Spirit our Helper.

The relationship between God and man is so much more personal in the NT due to the sacrifice of Jesus on the cross. People of the OT longed to know God as we can. They longed for their sin to be removed so they could fully embrace an intimate relationship with God.

This intimate relationship with God is only through faith in Jesus Christ. Jesus wants us to know God as our Father. He wants us to know an intimate, loving relationship with His Father. Jesus is welcoming us into His family. As a member of His family, we become children of His Father. God becomes our Father. The Holy Spirit serves as notice that we are children of God. In a sense, the Spirit is the adoption papers that seal us in our new family.

In the next two chapters, we will take a closer look at God as our Father and the role of the Holy Spirit. From here on, the pronoun 'He" will be used to refer to God. God has chosen the male gender to communicate with us. This does not make Him a man. This does not make him like a man. It does help us relate to Him in a personal way. The male pronoun makes God more personal. The male pronoun fits with God in the role of our Father.

CHAPTER 25

GOD THE FATHER

"For you are all sons of God through faith in
Christ Jesus…And because you are sons, God has
sent forth the Spirit of His Son into our hearts,
crying, 'Abba! Father!'"
Galatians 3:26, 4:6

Abba is the Aramaic word for Father (the word the Jews would probably have used). Father is the word the non-Aramaic speaker would use. 'Abba! Father!' is saying that God is the Father of Jew and non-Jew. He is the God of us all. He is the Father to believers of all nations. We can say that we all are "sons and daughters" of God. Very, very beautiful. Moreover, as sons and daughters of the same God, we are brothers and sisters.

Jesus stresses God to us as our Father. He tells us that our Father loves us just as much as He loves Jesus. We, who are in Jesus, are as beloved by the Father as Jesus, His only begotten Son. The Father loves you and me just as much as He loves Jesus.

For those who have had fathers who were abusive or non-existent, it may be difficult to relate to God as a Father. It may be difficult to feel God's Fatherly love. Your earthly father's "love," or lack of it, was painful. How do you relate to a heavenly Father, when your earthly father was bad?

You relate to God by letting God be God. It is baby steps of trust. You let His kindness and gentleness shine forth in your life one day at a time. Sometimes, one second at a time. God understands your struggles and is patient toward you. God will patiently, graciously and lovingly nurture the relationship so that you can safely call Him, Father. He loves you in a pure way.

When I think of a biblical character who had an abusive father, I think of King Hezekiah. His father was King Ahaz. Here is an example of Ahaz's treatment of his sons,

"But he walked in the way of the kings of Israel,
and even made his son pass through the fire,
according to the abominations of the nations
whom the Lord had driven out from before the
sons of Israel."
2 Kings 16:3

"Moreover, he burned incense in the valley of
Benhinnom, and burned his sons in fire…"
2 Chronicles 28:3

It was the practice of Canaanites, who lived in the nation of Judah, to offer sacrifices to their god, Molech.

The sacrifices involved tossing their sons into fire. It was not like burning them with a cigarette or a clothes iron. They were literally thrown into fire to burn alive. They burned to death. As the passages above describe, King Ahaz, Hezekiah's father, threw at least one of his sons into the fire as part of worship.

This was an abusive father. Hezekiah saw this. Hezekiah saw his brother(s) burned alive. He was impacted by this abuse. Yet, Hezekiah worshipped God. This is what we know about King Hezekiah,

> "He trusted in the Lord, the God of Israel; so that after him there was none like him among all the kings of Judah, nor among those who were before him."
> 2 Kings 18:5

With such an abusive father, how did Hezekiah have such a sweet relationship with God? How did he get past his father's abuse to know the love of the Lord? In one sense, the Bible does not tell us. In another sense, it does. King Hezekiah knew and trusted the stories of God's relationship to the fathers of Israel and the nation of Israel. He trusted that God was who God said He was as demonstrated in His faithfulness to the nation of Israel. He trusted that God was not like his father.

God was not like his father. God, as a Father, is closest to who King Hezekiah and OT believers knew as God. David in some of his psalms does refer to God as a Father.

God, as a Father to us, fulfills specific roles. His words are recorded in the Bible. He speaks to us. Jesus said,

> "He who does not love Me does not keep My words; and the word which you hear is not Mine, but the Father's who sent Me."
> John 14:24

The Apostle John opens his gospel with the picture of Jesus Christ, 'the only begotten from the Father' (John 1:14), as the word of God. The Father gave birth to the word of God. As we read the Bible, we are reading God the Father's words to us. He wishes to have a conversation with us. He wants to save us, heal us, walk with us and spend eternity with us.

It is the Father who blesses us,

> "Blessed be the God and Father of our Lord Jesus Christ, who has blessed us with every spiritual blessing in the heavenly places in Christ, just as He chose us in Him before the foundation of the world, that we should be holy and blameless before Him. In love He predestined us to adoption as sons through Jesus Christ to Himself, according to the kind intention of His will, to the praise of the glory of His grace, which He freely bestowed on us in the Beloved."
> Ephesians 1:3-6

The Apostle Paul states that the Father blesses us with 'every spiritual blessing.' It is not just some blessings but all. Every kindness bestowed upon man is an act of the Father. Every time you ponder the good in your life or the thing that went right in life, it is an act of the Father. He does it 'according to the kind intention of His will.' Have you considered the kindness of the Father toward you?

The ultimate act of kindness by the Father is:

> "For God so loved the world, that He gave His
> only begotten Son, that whoever believes in Him
> should not perish, but have eternal life."
> John 3:16

The Father's love sent Christ to the cross for our sins. A love for us. A love for you. It is a love that cares about our good.

> "Furthermore, we had earthly fathers to discipline
> us, and we respected them; shall we not much
> rather be subject to the Father of spirits, and live?
> For they disciplined us for a short time as seemed
> best to them, but He disciplines us for our good,
> that we may share His holiness."
> Hebrews 12:9, 10

The discipline of God as our Father is a scary topic. For some, discipline is synonymous with cruelty. God is not cruel. Yet, it is hard to separate our earthly father's cruelty from the fear of God's cruelty.

We need to understand God's discipline in light of His Son. To spare us the ultimate discipline for our sin, the Father's Son died on the cross. God so loves us that His Son bore the punishment for our sin. Ultimately, God chose to bear our punishment. He took His wrath out on Himself. He was cruel to Himself that He might extend kindness to us. I do not know if I will ever fully grasp what it cost God to show me tender love. It did cost Him.

God's discipline is not about satisfying His wrath. Or, satisfying His fury. Or, just because He can. God's discipline is about loving us so much that He wants us to partake of His blessings and His joy and His holiness. He wants us to be free to be all we were created to be. He seeks our joy not His own. It is about us and not about Him. It is about what He can give us, not what we can give Him. He fully accepts and loves us in Jesus Christ.

Understanding God as our Father is a wonderful gift. I have friends that can relate to God as a Father easily. I have other friends that find it more difficult. God is a loving Father to both. He is a Father that does not ask of us more than we can give. Rather, He gives all of Himself to us and tenderly loves us into the relationship.

If you find it difficult to relate to God as a Father, know that He understands and patiently waits for you. He is not going to forsake you. He is not waiting to harm you or abuse you. He will continue to pour out His unending love upon you. It is with tenderness that He deals with us, His children. He is committed to the fullness of our joy.

He is committed to always being with us. His Spirit, the Holy Spirit is the fulfillment of that promise. It is

through the Holy Spirit that we experience the presence of
God in our lives.

CHAPTER 26

GOD THE HOLY SPIRIT

"But the Helper, the Holy Spirit, whom the Father
will send in My name, He will teach you all things,
and bring to your remembrance all that I said to
you."
John 14:26

The Holy Spirit is probably the least known
personhood of God. Yet, it is the very person of God that
has the most interaction with us. The Holy Spirit is also
referred to as the Spirit of God and the Spirit of Christ.

The Greek word for Spirit is a neuter word and thus,
neither male nor female. The Spirt of God, in other words,
is neither male nor female. And, since the Holy Spirit is
God, that means God is not a man or a woman. It is
fascinating that God's most intimate communication with

His children is through the person of the Holy Spirit who is neither male nor female.

When Jesus spoke of the Spirit in John 14:26, He was trying to comfort His disciples because He would be leaving them soon. His death was imminent. He wanted them to know that while He was leaving, "the Helper, the Holy Spirit" would come. The Spirit that settled upon Jesus in His earthly ministry would be with them. He would be with all believers. The Apostle Paul wrote,

> "…the love of God has been poured out within
> our hearts through the Holy Spirit who was given
> to us."
> Romans 5:5

> "And because you are sons, God has sent forth the
> Spirit of His Son into our hearts, crying, "Abba!
> Father!"
> Galatians 4:6

The Spirit is the presence of God's love, God's Son and God the Father, in our lives. The Spirit is how God is with us. The Spirit is always with us. This means, God is always with us. Hear what God said to His servant Joshua just before the Israelites began to take possession of the Promised Land,

> "…I will be with you: I will not fail you or forsake
> you."
> Joshua 1:5

Hear the final words of Jesus to His disciples before He ascended into heaven,

"…I am with you always, even till the end of the age."
Matthew 28:20

God and Jesus' forever being with us is through the presence of the Holy Spirit in our lives. God promised Joshua and Jesus promises us that He "will not fail" or "forsake" us. God will be faithful and true to His love and commitment to us. While we least understand the work of the Holy Spirit, it is His presence in our lives day in and day out that allow us to serve the living God. He comforts and helps us.

How does the Holy Spirit bring the presence of God into our lives? He does it by indwelling believers (James 4:5). We, as believers, have the Spirit of God dwelling in us, guiding us in the things of God. This may sound a little like ghosts snatching bodies of the living. Well, it is not. Herein is the difference. The Holy Spirit does not need our body. The Holy Spirit indwells us that we might fully know God. The Holy Spirit indwells us that we might again taste the life we were created to live. It is God's promise to be with us forever.

God does not 'possess' us, but rather, it is a collaboration between the Spirit of God and the will of man. A relationship is about what is best for us. It is not about using us but rather, about us experiencing the fullness of life in Christ Jesus. It is a very beautiful bond. God wants us to know Him as He is.

The Apostle Paul tells us,

"For all who are being led by the Spirit of God,
these are sons of God."
Romans 8:14

As Romans 8:14 points out, the Holy Spirit leads us. He gives us direction into the will of our Father. He fills our hearts with the knowledge of our Father's love toward us. Some have called Him the Father's down payment of our permanent place in God's family.

There is so much to say about the Sprit's role in the life of believers. He commissions (Acts 13:4), commands (Acts 8:29), sanctifies (2 Thessalonians 2:13), convicts (John 16:8-11), gives gifts (1 Corinthians 12:11), and produces fruit (Galatians 5:22, 23), to just name a few of His duties. He also prays for us,

"And in the same way the Spirit also helps our weaknesses; for we do not know how to pray as we should, but the Spirit Himself intercedes for us with groanings too deep for words; and He who searches the hearts knows what the mind of the Spirit is, because He intercedes for the saints according to the will of God."
Romans 8:26, 27

The Holy Spirit prays for us. He prays for us according to the will of God. He intercedes for those "groanings" deep in our hearts that we cannot put into words. These verses tell us that as God searches our hearts, He seeks the mind of the Spirit. God the Father in heaven is having a conversation with His Spirit who resides in us. And, the conversation is about what is best for us. The Spirit who resides within us is pleading on our behalf for the blessings of the Father.

So, the Spirit not only causes us to remember God's spoken word to us, He also brings our spoken and unspoken words to God. His intimacy with God is brought to bear on our relationship with God. He brings that intimacy to us.

There is so much more to say about the Holy Spirit. Suffice to say, He is God, He is ever present with us, and He is neither male nor female. We refer to the Spirit as He because, Jesus and the Father are referred to as He. We are blessed that the Spirit has chosen to work on our behalf according to the will of God. He sees our struggles and He bears our pain. He understands pain. Christ was "a man of sorrows" (Isaiah 53:3). The Spirit knows the sorrows of Christ.

CHAPTER 27

JESUS CHRIST MAN OF SORROWS

"Pilate said to them, "Then what shall I do with
Jesus who is called Christ?" They all said, "Let
Him be crucified!" And he said, "Why, what evil
has He done?" But they kept shouting all the
more, saying, "Let Him be crucified!"
Matthew 27:22, 23

No one suffered evil more at the hands of men than
Jesus. Pilate asked a profound question, "Why, what evil
has He done?" They were not crucifying Christ because of
evil He had done. They were crucifying Christ because they
were evil.

As a child, when someone commits evil against us, we
assume we are the evil. The world evolves around us and

so something must be wrong with us. The reality is that there are evil people in the world.

Sin and sinners exist in our world. Evil is committed against us. Some of us may not experience it as harshly as others. Yet, we all experience it. We have discussed biblical characters that suffered at the hands of people that they should have been able to trust. They suffered evil from those who should have loved them. They needed protection from those who should have been their protectors.

When Jesus was arrested to be crucified, His closest disciples scattered. They deserted Him. It was by one of them that He was betrayed. Jesus understands the pain of abandonment and suffering at the hands of men. Christ could look past it for the joy set before Him and trust God.

The questions for us are, "Can we look past the evil of men and women and trust God?" "Can we let men be responsible for their evil?" Can we accept the fact that evil is part of our lives because of us and not God?"

You might be saying that that is easy for me to say. I do not know what evil you have endured. You are right and wrong. You are wrong that it is easy for me to say. God and I have had to work through quite a bit of pain in my heart. You are right that I do not know what evil you have endured. God does, though. And, He cares.

Christ suffered. His family had to flee their homeland because King Herod wanted him dead the day He was born (Matthew 2:16). He was rejected by His townspeople (Mark 6:4). In His early ministry, His family did not believe in Him (John 7:5). His nation's religious leaders sought His death

(Matthew 27:22, 23). Yes, Jesus will understand your sorrows.

Sorrow is part of life. Biblical characters suffered. We have discussed some, but there are others. Jacob was cheated and deceived by an uncle. Samson was deceived by a woman. Daniel, Meshach, Shadrach and Abednego were made eunuchs. Joash saw his grandmother kill all her son's children to gain power as the Queen of Judah. Joash lived because a sister hid him. Jeremiah was the weeping prophet. Paul after he became a Christian suffered much. All of these people were able to trust God. They were able to trust God because they knew God as God. They knew He was not like men.

Do any of these situations strike a nerve with you? If not, I am sure there is a life in the Bible that will. God understands the pain you have experienced at the hands of those who you should have been able to trust.

You can trust God. God is faithful to who He is. God is God. God is not a man. A wonderful, beautiful promise of God is,

> "for the Lamb in the center of the throne shall be
> their shepherd, and shall guide them to springs of
> the water of life; and God shall wipe every tear
> from their eyes."
> Revelation 7:17

God wants to comfort us. He wants to heal us of our pain. He wants to wipe every tear from our eyes. He wants us to know just how good He is.

CHAPTER 28

TASTE THE LORD

"O taste and see that the Lord is good; How
blessed is the man who takes refuge in Him!"
Psalm 34:8

What an invitation from a loving God. Taste and see
that the Lord is good. I think of samples that stores give
out to entice people to buy the product. The Psalmist is
asking us to taste God so that we can see that He is good.

Have you ever considered trying a taste of God? Have
you ever considered giving God a chance to show His love
toward you? Have you ever considered giving God your
deepest held secrets to find Him trustworthy and faithful?
Give Him a taste and see that He is good.

I took small tastes of God when I was trying to grow
my faith in God. I had a hard time believing that God cared
about what I cared about. I had a hard time believing He
cared about the smaller details of my life. I thought He

cared more about what I did than me. I was so wrong. So, I took God at His word,

"He who is faithful in a very little thing is faithful also in much; and he who is unrighteous in a very little thing is unrighteous also in much."
Luke 16:10

I tasted the Lord to see if He could be trusted in the little things. I tasted the Lord to see if He could be righteous in the little things. I found that the Lord is good. I found the Lord trustworthy and righteous in all His ways. I found that the Lord cared about the little things in my life that I cared about. He tasted good.

I do not want to paint this picture of the perfect life because you trust God. It has been difficult. God has helped me deal with a lot of pain. God has been so very good to me. He has been a place of safety and calm in the storms of life. It is hard to explain how you can have hope when you are in the depths of despair. Yet, because of God, one can.

I still have to remind myself to taste the Lord and see that He is good. In the struggles of living, it is easy to perceive God's abandonment as people have abandoned us. God, however, is ever present and ever faithful. He has stood by me even when I have lost sight of Him.

What do you have to gain by tasting the Lord? What do you have to gain by letting God show you how much He loves you? What do you have to lose if you do not?

One day, sitting in church, I noticed the cross in a new light. It had been moved and so it looked different. Later, I moved and looked at it from a new angle. It again looked different. The next day it was back in its normal spot and it looked different from the previous day. I pondered how every day is a new opportunity to look at the meaning of Christ's death on the cross for my life. There is always something new to discovery and taste. There is something new for you to discover and taste.

Can you let God be God? Can you allow yourself to know the God who bears the fruit of love, joy, peace, patience, kindness, goodness, faithfulness, gentleness and self-control? Can you trust the God who allowed His only begotten Son to die on the cross that you might know Him? Can you give God a taste?

God is God. God is not a man. God loves you with a pure and holy love. Taste and see that He is good.

APPENDIX A

EXPRESSING FAITH IN CHRIST

"For by grace you have been saved through faith;
and that not of yourselves, it is the gift of God;"
Ephesians 2:8

If you died and came before God, and He asked why He should let you into heaven, are you able to say because of what Christ did on the cross? Because of the grace found in Christ? Christ said,

"If anyone wishes to come after Me, let him deny himself, and take up his cross daily, and follow Me.
For whoever wishes to save his life shall lose it,
but whoever loses his life for My sake, he is the one who will save it.'
Luke 9:23-24

Faith in Christ is not just about forgiveness of sin. It is also about living God's way for your life. It is denying self for the life of Christ. It is a commitment to a relationship with God with Him first. When this happens, Christ promised that the Spirit of God would come and empower us to live for Christ.

> "I have been crucified with Christ; and it is no longer I who live, but Christ lives in me; and the life which I now live in the flesh I live by faith in the Son of God, who loved me, and delivered Himself up for me."
> Galatians 2:20

Are you ready to accept this grace with faith? Would you like to declare your faith in Jesus Christ for your life? Do you want a relationship with God?

One way we express faith is to talk to God through prayer. Prayer is communicating with God. The prayer which follows is a guide to help you express your faith in God's grace and love for you, accept the forgiveness of your sin through Christ's death, and receive the power of the Spirit of God in your life.

Dear Jesus Christ, I am a sinner. There are things I have done that I regret. Thank you that as an act of your grace and love you came to pay the penalty for my sins and that there is nothing I need to do to be forgiven. I accept Your death and resurrection on my behalf. I ask in faith that You be my life. I thank you that the Spirit of God lives in me now and will cause me to grow to be more and more like You. Amen.

"Behold, God is my salvation, I will trust and not
be afraid; For the Lord God is my strength and
song, and He has become my salvation."
Isaiah 12:2

"And this is the confidence which we have before
Him, that, if we ask anything according to His will,
He hears us. And if we know that He hears us in
whatever we ask, we know that we have the
requests which we have asked from Him."
1 John 5:14, 15

With that decision, God wants you to grow in your new faith and new relationship with Him. Three very good ways to continue growing in your faith are through reading the Bible, gathering with other believers and journaling.

Reading the Bible. Choose a good study Bible. New American Standard translation is recommended, though are several good translations. Begin reading one of the four gospels, Matthew, Mark, Luke or John; biographies of Jesus in the New Testament.

Find a good church. A good church believes in salvation through Jesus Christ alone; no additional works are required. The church teaches the word of God is without error and inspired. If you cannot find a church, please feel free to e-mail mlyon2004@gmail.com. Every effort will be made to find someone who can help you.

Journal your decision and new faith. Keep your testimony of faith close by for you and to share with others. You will want to revisit your decision to follow Christ as a reminder of the commitment you made. It is your story of faith.

Jesus promises us,

> "My sheep hear My voice, and I know them, and they follow Me; and I give eternal life to them, and they shall never perish; and no one shall snatch them out of My hand. My Father, who has given them to Me, is greater than all; and no one is able to snatch them out of the Father's hand."
> John 10:27-29

You have eternal spiritual life in Jesus Christ! You have a relationship with God you cannot lose! Welcome to the family of God.

ABOUT THE AUTHOR

Mary was a senior in college when she committed her life to the Lordship of Christ. Upon graduation, rather than pursue her engineering career, she became a missionary.

Often she was asked why she gave up the money and the opportunities offered her as a woman engineer. Her response was always that she did not give up anything. If God wanted her to be an engineer again one day, she would be.

Twenty years later she was getting her Master's Degree in Engineering Management and her Professional Engineering License in Mechanical Engineering. Earlier she had received her Master's Degree in Counseling.

Mary would say the path she followed is the one God planned for her. He has walked with her the whole way. One of her favorite comments is from The Hiding Place by Corrie Ten Boom – There are no ifs in the will of God.

Contact information:

Mlyon2004@gmail.com

Books by Mary L. Lyon

He Walks With Us
It is about how God takes His children by the hand, walking with them in His love, forgiveness and truth.

Forty Years Later
God's Faithfulness Across Generations
The Christian life involves struggles. The stories of Bible characters guide us in our struggles.

Jesus Christ Evangelistic Series

Jesus Christ
Why
A succinct presentation of the need for faith in Jesus Christ as Savior and Lord.

Jesus Christ
God's Relationship of Grace
Discusses the relationship we have with God through Jesus Christ in a Bible study format.

www.ingramcontent.com/pod-product-compliance
Lightning Source LLC
Chambersburg PA
CBHW060934140726
47996CB00001B/491